Global Communications

Nikola Tesla' s Death Ray
And The
Columbia Space Shuttle Disaster

Sean Casteel
with
Commander X

Nikola Tesla's Death Ray and the Columbia Space Shuttle Disaster

Introduction

Nothing fills me with a greater sense of pride than our country's space program. It's no secret that since I was a child I have been fascinated by the stars and planets and the mysteries the universe awaiting those whose imaginations stretch beyond the confines of our world. I had often dreamed that someday I would be able to travel into space and see with my own eyes that which only a privileged few have been lucky enough to see. However, with the exception of a couple of top secret experiments I was lucky enough to be able to participate in, my feet, unfortunately, have remained firmly planted on good old terra firma.

As the years have gone by I have watched mankind take the first faltering steps into space. At first it consisting of shooting people into orbit in what amounted to nothing more than simple tin cans filled with oxygen, to increasingly sophisticated spacecraft that eventually took us to the dusty surface of the moon.

After the moon, the hope was that the next logical step would be to travel and land on the planet Mars - but we would need a more complex and sophisticated system to achieve this goal. We would need a space station in permanent orbit around the Earth, and a way to quickly and efficiently ferry goods and supplies from the surface and into space. That was, at least, the original purpose for the space shuttle, sort of a "space truck" to get stuff into orbit cheaper and faster than multi-stage rockets.

Unfortunately, politics, a lack of imagination, and an inability to see man's ultimate destiny in the stars, forced budget cut-backs that slowed the development of the space program to a crawl. The space shuttle, instead of being just one of many spacecraft that would be available for space exploration, became the only vehicle available to the United States to send astronauts into orbit. This sad state of affairs has persisted for many years now and as the shuttle fleet grows increasingly older, accidents, like that which befell Challenger in 1986, become more likely to occur.

Now, another tragedy has overtaken the space shuttle program with the death of seven brave astronauts and the destruction of the oldest spacecraft in the fleet, Columbia. There is no sugarcoating the realities of space flight—it's dangerous work and people will die. But throughout recorded history exploration has always been fraught with perils and dangers because the rewards of discovery far outweigh the risks. Thank God for the brave souls who risk their very lives to continually push the envelope of knowledge.

The fact that exploration is dangerous doesn't bother me. The thrill of satisfying ones curiosity to see what lies just around the comer is built into our very souls. It is what has driven us as a species for countless generations, and hopefully will continue to drive us for many more.

What does bother me is the fact that the space shuttle Columbia may not have broken up on re-entry because of some yet unknown structural breakdown. Instead, as some are now beginning to suspect, Columbia suffered a catastrophic accident due to the deliberate application of a weapon of mass destruction that up until now, has been kept wrapped up tight in the top secret, black budgets of the world's super-powers.

Eyewitness testimony, shocking videos, and digital photographs taken by an amateur astronomer could be the evidence needed to prove that Columbia was destroyed by a beam of energy that was so powerful that it literally disintegrated the shuttle's atomic matrix.

Rumors of the "Death Ray" have bounced around for years in the halls and around the drinking fountains of the government and military. Research on the military applications of lasers, electricity, radio frequency waves, particle beams, etc. is nothing new. The British as far back as the early 1920's conducted top-secret experiments with Death Rays, so the concept and research on this technology has been science fact for quite awhile now.

But there is one name that has become synonymous with the death ray and its potentials—that name is Nikola Tesla. Tesla, well known as the father of AC current and the creator of our modern electrical system, announced on his 78th birthday in 1934, his concept of an invention "powerful enough to destroy 10,000 planes 250 miles away." Tesla also claimed that his "Death Beam" could kill one person or one hundred without leaving a single trace."

What made Tesla's Death Ray plausible from all the others being currently worked on was that he found a way to deliver enough power to the energy beam to make it effective over great distances. But in the early 1930's, technology had not yet caught up with Tesla's ideas and his death beam remained a dream.

The story of the Death Ray does not end with the death of Nikola Tesla. As we now know, there was interest in Tesla's ideas and the theft of many of his secret papers by the U.S. and Soviet governments prove the point. Now, years later, it appears that Tesla's Death Beam has become a chilling reality. The questions, however, remain the same: Who has the Death Ray; has it been used in the past; and was it responsible for the destruction of Columbia; and why?

Commander X

Chapter One

The Columbia Tragedy

The tragic loss of the Space Shuttle Columbia and its seven astronauts will live forever in the memory of the American people. While the actual cause may never be known beyond a shadow of a doubt, it is nevertheless possible that an outside force acted upon the spaceship, an outside force which may have been set into motion many decades ago by the work of legendary inventor Nikola Tesla and the shadowy scientists who followed in his wake.

But first, a review of the fateful events of February 1, 2003.

Columbia's Final Minutes

As reported in the February 10, 2003 issue of *Time Magazine*, the final 45 minutes of the Columbia's descent to death went like this:

"Commander Rick Husband fired his deorbit engines at 8:15 AM Eastern Time when the ship was high over the Indian Ocean. Half an hour and

1

half a world-later, it hit the edges of the atmosphere just north of Hawaii at an altitude of about 400,000 feet. Shortly after, a faint pink glow began to surround the ship, as atmospheric friction caused temperatures to rise to between 750 and 3,000 degrees across various parts of the spacecraft's underbelly.

"The astronauts, busy monitoring their deceleration, temperature, hydraulics and more, didn't have much time to watch the light show play out, and by the time the pink glow brightened from faint pink to bright pink to plasma white, the ship had arced around the planet into thick air and daylight.

"On the ground, things were smooth too. At Cape Canaveral the conditions were perfect for landing, with temperatures in the low 70s and a light breeze blowing, well within NASA's wind limits. The families of some of the seven crew members had already been shown to the runway, assembling for their close-up view of the touchdown."

But into that idyllic picture, the problems seemed to come from nowhere.

As the ship was flying over San Francisco, several technical malfunctions began to happen in rapid succession, with many of the shuttle's sensors suddenly ceasing to transmit data back to Mission Control. As the Columbia reached the skies over Texas, spacecraft communicator Charlie Hobaugh attempted to alert the seven crew members. Commander Rick Husband began to respond to Hobaugh, but his transmission went dead before the astronaut could complete his first sentence.

Hobaugh tried repeatedly to re-establish contact but even the computer downlink had failed, and soon the ship was coming apart over the Dallas-Fort Worth area. When the shuttle failed to land on schedule at 9:16 AM, NASA began a search and rescue effort.

The Beginnings Of A Cover-Up?

"With reports coming back of a debris field that stretched from eastern Texas to Louisiana, and possibly even further, NASA put out the somewhat disingenuous word that fumes from the fragments could be dangerous and that people who found them should leave them where they lay and alert the authorities—as if any toxic fuel could have survived the heat of re-entry," *Time* reported.

Was that initial warning from NASA about

people not touching the fragments they found an early attempt to cover-up just exactly what caused the Columbia to crash? Even *Time Magazine* seems to distrust NASA's real intentions there, calling the warning "disingenuous," and one cannot help but speculate that the wreckage could have held clues vital to understanding whether a top-secret particle beam weapon was the real culprit in what happened to space shuttle Columbia and the seven brave astronauts who entrusted their lives to the integrity of the ship.

The specter of terrorism also reared its ugly head, with the media in general responding to what was a widespread concern among many Americans.

The terrorism theory was discounted early on, however, because it seemed unlikely that even the most dedicated terrorist could bring it off. Theoretically, a shoulder-launched missile could shoot down an aircraft, but no such missile could have reached the altitude Columbia was at when it disintegrated. Smuggling an explosive onboard was also not taken seriously because security around the shuttle was simply so tight as to make that impossible.

While *Time* and other news sources poohpoohed the terrorism theory, again the trail leads back to the possibility of a secret particle beam weapon, one able to fire out past the altitude limits of a more mundane kind of missile and wreak the havoc that brought Columbia down from the skies that day over Texas.

Mysterious Photographs Surface

On February 3, 2003, the day after the Columbia disaster, *The San Francisco Chronicle* ran an article that described odd images photographed near the shuttle.

David Perlman, the newspaper's science editor, wrote that, "A San Francisco amateur astronomer who photographs the space shuttles whenever their orbits carry them over the Bay Area has captured five strange and provocative images of the shuttle Columbia just as it was re-entering the Earth's atmosphere before dawn Saturday.

"The pictures, taken with a Nikon-880 digital camera on a tripod, reveal what appear to be bright electrical phenomena flashing around the track of the shuttle's passage, but the photographer, who asked not to be identified, will not make them public immediately. 'They clearly record an electrical discharge like a lightning bolt flashing past, and I was snapping the pictures almost exactly when the Columbia may have begun breaking up during re-entry,' he said.

"The photographer invited *The Chronicle* to view the photos on his computer screen Saturday night, and they are indeed puzzling. They show a bright scraggly flash of orange light, tinged with pale purple, and shaped somewhat like a deformed L. The flash appears to cross Columbia's dim contrail, and at that precise point, the contrail abruptly brightens and appears thicker and somewhat twisted, as if it were wobbling."

The photographer said, "I couldn't see the discharge with my own eyes, but it showed up clear and bright on the film when I developed it. But I'm not going to speculate about what it might be."

The Mystery Deepens

On February 5, *The San Francisco Chronicle* ran a follow-up article by Sabin Russell, a staff writer for the paper.

"Top investigators of the Columbia space shuttle disaster are analyzing a startling photograph—snapped by an amateur astronomer from a San Francisco hillside—that appears to show a purplish electrical bolt of unknown origin striking the craft as it streaked across the California sky. The digital image is one of five snapped by the shuttle buff at roughly 5:53 AM Saturday as sensors on the doomed orbiter began showing the first indications of trouble. Seven minutes later, the craft broke up in flames over Texas.

"Although there are several possible benign explanations for the image—such as a barely perceptible jiggle of the camera as it took the time exposure—NASA's zeal to examine the photo demonstrates the lengths at which the agency is going to tap the resources of ordinary Americans in solving the puzzle. Late Tuesday, NASA dispatched former shuttle astronaut Tammy Jernigan, now a manager at Lawrence Livermore Laboratories, to the San Francisco home of the astronomer to examine his digital images and to take the camera itself to Mountain View, where it was to be transported by a NASA T-38 jet to Houston this morning.

"A *Chronicle* reporter was present when the astronaut arrived. First seeing the image on a large computer screen, she had one word: "Wow.""

Jernigan quizzed the photographer on technical details of how the photos were shot. In the most critical of the photos, a glowing purple rope of light corkscrews down toward the plasma trail, appears to pass behind it, then cuts sharply toward it from below. As it merges with the plasma trail, the streak itself brightens for a distance, and then fades.

Jernigan said, "It certainly appears very anomalous. We sure will be very interested in taking a very hard look at this."

Did some unknown weapon cause the mysterious flash? Is that why NASA sent a former astronaut to view the images, then chartered a special jet to fly the camera itself to Houston? That tantalizing possibility is one of many that this report will deal with.

The Atmosphere Itself Is A Mystery

As reported on February 11, 2003, on well-known abductee and author Whitley Strieber's website, www.unknowncountry.co , "The space shuttle Columbia broke up in a mysterious area of the upper atmosphere called the ionosphere, which is filled with free electrons—or ions—that can reflect electromagnetic energy, producing strange electrical effects like 'elves,' 'sprites' and 'blue jets.' Until recently, these were dismissed as illusions seen by tired airline pilots. An amateur astronomer took a photo showing purple light near the shuttle's trail as it passed through this area. This middle atmosphere is too high for balloons and airplanes, but too low for satellites, so it's been little studied.

"We're discovering the middle atmosphere has got a lot of electrical phenomena," says Walt Lyons, of FMA Research. "The key message here is that there may be more things going on up there that we just don't understand or have no inkling of yet. The research that we've been able todo has made us realize it's even weirder than we thought. There may be other things that happen up there that we just don't know about. Maybe we just encountered a new phenomenon the hard way."

And could that "new phenomenon" be the Death Ray invented by Nikola Tesla? Is his technology still so advanced that our current scientists cannot determine its presence by the normal methods used to analyze such things?

NIKOLA TESLA'S DEATH RAY AND THE COLUMBIA SPACE SHUTTLE DISASTER

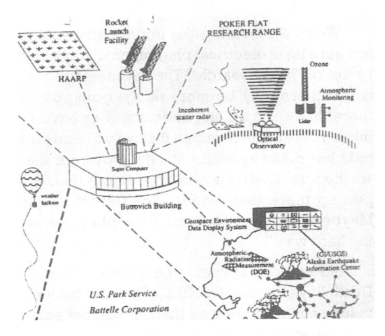

HAARP and Poker Flats Research Facility

Chapter Two

Tesla's Deadly Death Ray

From the account of the Columbia tragedy, we next flashback to September 22, 1940, when an article appeared in *The New York Times* in which Nikola Tesla first revealed his "Death Ray" to the public. The entire text of the article follows in order to give the reader a feel for the historical importance of Tesla's announcement.

The article was headlined *Death Ray For Planes.*

(snip) "Nikola Tesla, one of the truly great inventors, who celebrated his eighty-fourth birthday on July 10, tells the writer that he stands ready to divulge to the United States government the secret of his 'teleforce,' of which he said, 'Airplane motors would be melted at a distance of 250 Miles, so that an invisible "Chinese Wall of Defense" would be built around the country against any enemy attack by an enemy air force, no matter how large.'

NIKOLA TESLA'S DEATH RAY AND THE COLUMBIA SPACE SHUTTLE DISASTER

"This 'teleforce' is based on an entirely new principle of physics that no one has ever dreamed about, different from the principles embodied in his inventions relating to the transmission of electrical power from a distance, for which he has received a number of basic patents.

"This new type of force Mr. Tesla said would operate through a beam one-hundred-millionth of a square centimeter in diameter, and could be generated from a special plant that would cost no more than $2,000,000 and would take only about three months to construct. A dozen such plants, located at strategic points along the coast, according to Mr. Tesla, would be enough to defend the country against all aerial attack.

"The beam would melt any engine, whether diesel or gasoline, and would also ignite the explosives aboard any bomber. No possible defense against it could be devised, he asserts, as the beam would be all penetrating through wood and metal alike.

High Vacuum Eliminated

"The beam, he states, involves four new inventions, two of which already have been tested. One of these is a method and apparatus that eliminates the need for a 'high vacuum'; a second is a process for producing 'very great electrical force'; the third is a method of amplifying this force, and the fourth is a new method for producing 'a tremendous repelling electrical force.' This would be the projector, or the gun of the system.

"The voltage for propelling the beam to its objective, according to the inventor, will attain a potential of 80,000,000 volts. With this enormous voltage, he said, microscopic electrical particles of matter will be catapulted on their mission of defensive destruction. He has been working on this invention, he added, for many years and has made a number of improvements on it.

"Mr. Tesla makes one important stipulation. Should the government decide to take up his offer, he would go to work on it at once, but they would have to trust him. He would suffer 'no interference from experts who don't know what they are doing.'

"In ordinary times, such a condition would very likely interpose an insuperable obstacle. But times being what they are, and with the nation getting ready to spend billions on national defense, at the same time taking in consideration the reputation of Mr. Tesla as an inventor who always was many years ahead of his time, the question arises whether it may not be advisable to take Mr. Tesla at his word and commission him to go ahead with his 'teleforce' plant."

Such A Device "Invaluable"

"After all, $2,000,000 would be relatively a very small sum compared with what is at stake. If Mr. Tesla really fulfills his promise, the results achieved would be truly staggering. Not only would it save billions now planned for air defense, by making the country absolutely impregnable against any air attack, but it also would save many more billions in property that would otherwise be surely destroyed no matter how strong the defenses are, as witness current events in England.

"Take, for example, the Panama Canal. No matter how strong the defense, a suicide squadron of dive-bombers, according to some experts, might succeed in getting through and cause such damage that would make the Canal unusable, in which our Navy might find itself bottled up.

"Considering the probabilities in the case, even if the chances were a hundred thousand to one against Mr. Tesla, the odds would still be largely in favor of taking a chance and spending $2,000,000. In the opinion of the writer, who has known Mr, Tesla for many years, the authorities in charge of building national defense should at once look into the matter. The sum is insignificant compared to the magnitude of the stake."

(snip)

The Authorities Indeed

The **New York Times** writer, whose byline unfortunately did not appear with the article, seems to very much respect and admire Tesla, saying that the inventor retains his "full intellectual vigor" at the advanced age of eighty-four and urging the powers that be to take an enlightened interest in Tesla's claims that he could make the country impregnable against attack by air by method of his Death Ray.

It is interesting to note also that Tesla was promoting the invention at the time as a weapon of defense, not as an offensive weapon of mass destruction. Along with the billions in defense funds and property that would be saved by the use of Tesla's Death Ray, one can only think of the lives that might have been saved, like say at Pearl Harbor the year following the article's publication. Tesla claimed that he could have the device up and running in three months if he had proper funding, which would have been in plenty of time to repel the Japanese surprise attack that set in motion the U.S. entry into World War II.

But it is with the use of the Death Ray as an offensive weapon that this report is concerned. Even though Tesla never brought his "teleforce" device to complete fruition in his own lifetime, is it possible that others have taken the inventor's ideas and succeeded in creating an offensive weapon, the powers of which we still can only speculate? And was just such a weapon used to bring down Columbia?

Tesla touted the Death Ray as a means to bring down aircraft, and perhaps we have already seen a demonstration of how that was accomplished all too well.

Nikola Tesla: The New Wizard of the West
From Pearson's Magazine, May 1899

Chapter Three

Death in the Upper Atmosphere:

Who is Responsible?

There is a long history of United States rocket disasters that stretches back to the 1980s. According to certain experts studying the problem, the idea that the Russians are behind the lost rockets and are achieving their ends by use of the Death Ray first developed by Nikola Tesla is not totally outside the realm of possibility.

The following material is provided on the Internet at a site called "Iron Eagles," with no single author credited for the online article. The anonymous author paints a fascinating picture of covert Russian sabotage of our rockets as well as a glimpse into Soviet penetration of our scientific community.

Russians Draw A Line In The Sand

The report begins by recalling comments made by the late Soviet Premier Nikita Khrushchev, who attempted to intimidate the

American people by saying, "We shall bury you." He also threatened that "The U.S. will eventually fly the Communist red flag." The author then declares that a large number of American scientists, politicians, bankers and corporate executives are "strategically and actively supporting and cooperating with the Soviet Union. In short, they are providing the Kremlin with the shovel to bury the U.S."

Leaving politics aside for the moment, the report moves on to talk about the Russian alleged sabotage of eight U.S. rockets over a 19-month period.

"There is clear evidence to prove that the U.S. rockets were deliberately assaulted and annihilated. The Atlas-Centaur, which blew up over Cape Canaveral, Florida, on March 26, 1987, carried a very important strategic defense satellite. It was the target of a Soviet electromagnetic attack.

"Beginning with the explosion of a Titan-35-D rocket in 1985, then the destruction of the Space Shuttle Challenger on January 28, 1986, the U.S. has lost eight rockets in mysterious accidents. This chain of accidents is unheard of in the history of U.S. space programs.

NIKOLA TESLA'S DEATH RAY AND THE COLUMBIA SPACE SHUTTLE DISASTER

"The *Washington Times* of March 27, 1987, reported, 'The latest devastating NASA failure cost taxpayers $161 million. The 137-foot rocket veered off course at an altitude of 14,250 feet.' The destroyed rocket had many functions, one of which was to provide vital strategic communications links to be used in the event of war. The 'Fleet SatCom' satellites controlled by the U.S. Navy are used to communicate with command centers and ships at sea and with fighters and ground forces stationed around the globe. These satellites also serve as an emergency communication link between the President and the field officials posted all over the world."

Did Lightning Strike More Than Once?

Having established the crucial military nature of the lost rockets and satellites, the report moves on to discuss the dubious theory that natural lightning caused the accidents.

As reported in *The Washington Post* on March 28, 1987, "Of more than 2,000 rockets launched from Cape Canaveral in more than three decades, only one is known to have been hit by lightning after launch. When an unexpected bolt of lightning barely touched a Saturn V rocket, the electrical system immediately returned to nominal and the crew continued on their mission."

NIKOLA TESLA'S DEATH RAY AND THE COLUMBIA SPACE SHUTTLE DISASTER

Nevertheless, in the case of the 1987 Atlas-Centaur incident, NASA announced it had been demolished by "something like a bolt of lightning."

Soon after, the **Post** declared that, "A four-stroke flash of lightning struck within two miles of the launch pad at the Cape, seconds before the rocket's steerable engines swerved 'hard over,' pushing it off course and sending it tumbling. That flash was observed between 48 and 53 seconds after launch, at 40 millisecond intervals."

The Iron Eagles report next quotes John Busse, director of Flight Assurance at Goddard Space Flight Center.

"Just before the rocket veered off, traveling faster than the speed of sound, a microphone in the nose cone detected a sound that drove it 'offscale.' Batteries in the Atlas first-stage and the Centaur second-stage showed major electrical transients of variations. The rocket's digital computer unit then issued commands to the engines that sent the rocket tumbling out of control."

This is simply the high-tech explanation for what went wrong.

"There certainly are a lot of strong indications

that electromagnetic phenomena are associated with the failure of Atlas-Centaur 67," Busse said.

"It could be lightning, a vehicle induced static charge, and other things I'm not smart enough to talk about."

NASA is aware of the Soviet electromagnetic attacks, the report flatly declares, but no NASA people will admit to this because, if they did, they could be fired by proSoviet elements within the U.S. government. Whether or not that is simple political paranoia, it is still evident that some kind of cover-up was firmly in place.

For instance, on April 17, 1987, *The Washington Times* stated that, "The factfinding committee for the rocket disaster discovered that nine lightning strikes hit the Alpha-Centaur before it broke apart." The odds are slight, the report reasons, for more than one natural lightning stroke to directly hit a rocket's tiny nose cone within a few seconds. Therefore, the idea of nine such strikes is simply ludicrous.

The newspaper also reported, "Investigators are at a loss to explain how the lightning strikes caused the onboard computers to send a hardover command to the Atlas booster engine and caused the rocket to mysteriously veer off course and out of control. It was as if it received a special encoded command from the ground. Natural lightning would have simply knocked out the computer and caused it to immediately lose power to some extent, but it never issues any commands to the engines."

Tesla And Manmade Lightning

So where did the lightning come from if it wasn't of the "natural" variety? The report next puts forth the claim that Tesla-created technology was a vital part of the picture.

"Manmade lightning, or the Soviet Scalar Weapons System, uses a technique developed by Nikola Tesla, a great scientist and inventor. As the explosion of eight U.S. rockets that has occurred since August 25, 1985, shows, scalar weapons can easily destroy rockets in flight.

The events related to the demolition of the Atlas-Centaur rocket provide strong evidence of the use of Tesla-scalar weapons. Tesla spent most of his life generating controlled lightning and any high school student could obtain a Tesla coil and generate lightning on an experimental scale."

After accusing the Russians of beginning to use devices called Tesla Magnifying Transmitters in 1976, the report next asserts that soon after

NIKOLA TESLA'S DEATH RAY AND THE COLUMBIA SPACE SHUTTLE DISASTER

"U.S. military intelligence satellites reported sighting monster lightning bolts over the U.S.S.R. The 'super bolts' were reportedly thousands of times more powerful than natural lightning, up to about 10 trillion watts. Prior to these U.S. satellite sightings, the most powerful natural lightning bolts ever recorded were only 10 billion watts."

Another group of scientists claimed that a Soviet Tesla Magnifying Transmitter was in operation at Gomel, in Russia, and "has been known to emit alone, or in conjunction with another facility, Extremely Low Frequency (ELF) signals at a strength of up to 40 million watts." The scientists also said that there is another Soviet-controlled Tesla Magnifying Transmitter in the eastern part of Havana, Cuba.

Suspiciously enough, just before the first of the eight rockets was destroyed in August of 1985, a group of Soviet scientists withdrew a paper on microwave generation, which was scheduled to be presented at an international conference in Europe. The scientists said they had recently learned that their documents were declared to be classified.

The rest of the Iron Eagles report consists mostly of unfounded claims that there is a "surrender mentality" operating in the current government and scientific research communities, meaning that there is a great deal of covert co-operation with the Russians, which includes things like our own space program. The Russians continue to use secret Tesla technology to shoot down our rockets, maybe even the Columbia itself, and meanwhile the U.S does nothing to resist the attacks either publicly or behind the scenes. The reader is of course invited to draw his own conclusions.

Another Source Is Heard From

Another article appeared on the Internet, this time written by Jamie Adams. Adams also discussed the possibility that Tesla's Death Ray had brought down both the Challenger and the Columbia.

"The Russian Scalar Technology," Adams wrote, "including Particle Beam Weapons, and the relation to the possibility of the Challenger shuttle explosion via the Electromagnetic Pulse Weapon was, of course, a derivative of the Tesla Death Ray and/or the Tower of Tesla that was supposed to be used in strategic places to accomplish this feat. Upon entrance into our atmosphere, entering this invisible blanket of 'electromagnetic pulse' would undoubtedly fry all circuitry within any aircraft and, as studies suggest, this would include aircraft of extraterrestrial origin as well."

As regards the Columbia crash on February 1, 2003, Adams wrote, "You'll notice there was a corona discharge around the shuttle as it was entering the atmosphere, which is a side-effect of the EMP blanket observed by American scientists and wellknown by and experimented with and possibly perfected by Russian scientists since the Cold War. The EMP blanket can follow the curvature of the ozone and inner atmospheric pressure," Adams continued, "as a natural guideline, for several hundreds of miles. It can be invisible, using the pulse method, or it can actually be seen as what is referred to as 'the Death Ray,' which will protrude for several miles in atomic adhesion. It will look like a fat laser beam but is, in all actuality, such a concentration of electromagnetic control in correlation with gravity/antigravity manipulation that for a small fraction of what is considered human 'real time,' time is fragmented and actually penetrated, thereby leaving a questionable gap in the space/time continuum.

"This technology can actually supercede space and time to get to its designated target, which is suspected of being how UFO craft get from point A to point B, by distorting gravity to an extent of gravitational confusion and exerting [an object] to a preordained position of choice."

Having explained some of the complicated science involved, Adams then says, "Consider what Nikola Tesla accomplished in the 1800s that still isn't perfected today (wireless communications, etc.), yet was not only prognosticated, but actually attempted until the relaxation of trusted funds ultimately diluted any further experimentation with his best ideas."

This is another way of expressing the standard regret one often feels regarding Tesla: in spite of his genius, there just never seemed to be enough money. But did the Russians decide to spend as much as was necessary to complete Tesla's research into the Death Ray? In trying to build such an invincible weapon, one can be assured that money is no object.

An Important Clarification

It is not our intention to point the finger at the current Russian government. For instance, it should be remembered that the string of sabotaged rocket incidents began in 1985, just as the Cold War was beginning to thaw. It is perhaps more plausible to assume that if a Death Ray was used, it was a weapon that had fallen into the hands of a shadow Russian government or even hostile rogues who had split off from some political organization. As the government changed hands in that period, any number of weapons may have been stolen and put to a use the true Russian government never intended.

Dramatic photos of Columbia breaking up as it passes over Texas.

NIKOLA TESLA'S DEATH RAY AND THE COLUMBIA SPACE SHUTTLE DISASTER

Chapter Four

Origins of Particle Weaponry

Tim Swartz is an author and an Emmy Award-winning television news producer who has written numerous books on the paranormal, as well as the classic work *The Lost Journals of Nikola Tesla* (Global Communications). In an interview conducted exclusively for this book, Swartz spoke about Tesla's early years, his possible connection to the Tunguska explosion of 1908, and the history of his legendary invention, the Death Ray.

The Early Years Of Nikola Tesla

Swartz began by giving some biographical data on Tesla.

"Nikola Tesla was born in what is now Yugoslavia," Swartz said. "He was born to Serbian parents who lived near the western edge of the Austria-Hungarian Empire. He was born at midnight between July 9 and 10, 1856 to Georgina (Djuka) Mandic and the Reverend Milutin Tesla.

NIKOLA TESLA'S DEATH RAY AND THE
COLUMBIA SPACE SHUTTLE DISASTER

Tesla always said he inherited his intelligence from his mother who he called 'brilliant.'

"Right from the very beginning," Swartz continued, "Tesla showed a knack for thinking up things, little inventions. From the beginning he had his heart set on becoming an engineer. He seemed to have a keen mind towards putting things together or coming up with new ways of doing traditional things. Tesla exhibited a strange trait; he had an abnormal ability to visualize scenes, people, and things so vividly that he was often unsure what was real and what was imaginary. He attended the renowned Austrian Polytechnic School at Gratz where he studied mechanical and electrical engineering. In 1884 Tesla immigrated to the United States and, with a letter of introduction from Charles Batchelor, the English engineer who managed the Continental Edison Company in Europe, Tesla went to New York to seek out Thomas Edison.

"He came to the United States seeking to work with Thomas Edison. Tesla was a great admirer of Edison, and both men were interested in engineering, electricity and ways that it could be transmitted. Tesla was eager to discuss his ideas of an AC motor with Edison because he was certain that a man of such great genius as Edison would immediately grasp the positive implications of AC.

"Most electricians of the time," Swartz went on, "were thinking of electricity in terms of electric lights and trolley cars. Tesla envisioned it as the means to unite cities and distant villages, to span whole continents. At that time Edison had a DC power service that stretched out over New York City. It wasn't a very efficient system because DC is rapidly diminished by resistance along transmission wires, making it unsuitable for electrification over distances greater than a mile.

"The day Tesla arrived for his interview with Thomas Edison, the manager of a shipping firm had called to remind Edison that the **SS Oregon** had been tied up for days awaiting electrical repairs on an ill-built system installed by Edison's company. That was a particularly bad day for Edison because he had all of his engineers out fixing other problems, so he turned to Tesla and asked him if he could 'fix a ship's lighting plant?'

"Tesla said he could and Edison sent him to work right away. Not only did Tesla fix the **SS Oregon's** problem in less than 24 hours, but he also worked on the ships dynamo's to improve their efficiency, despite the fact they were designed for direct current. Edison was extremely impressed and immediately hired Tesla.

"But the two men were probably a little too much alike in personality, because they never got along. Tesla saw Edison as an uneducated tinkerer, while Tesla was inclined to approach things mathematically. Edison would just start throwing things together along with his team in his laboratory just to see what would happen, while Tesla was more meticulous and thought out things very carefully before he even started the construction phase of any of his inventions.

"So right away," Swartz said, "the two men clashed, and Tesla eventually left the Edison Company to go out on his own. With the help of backing by several financiers, Tesla started the *Tesla Electric Lighting Company* which eventually led to the development of the AC motor and the modem AC electrical system."1

A Mystery In Siberia

Swartz next filled in the background of Nikola Tesla's possible involvement in the fabled Tunguska explosion in Siberia.

"The Tunguska Siberia explosion occurred on June 30, 1908," Swartz said, "A massive explosion of unknown origin struck an isolated part of

Siberia, destroying miles of forest, whole herds of reindeer, and even some small villages. To this day no one really knows what caused this event.

"At the same time as the Tunguska explosion," Swartz explained, "Robert Perry was making his second attempt to reach the North Pole. Meanwhile, Tesla was having terrible money problems. His main financial sources had backed out, and Tesla was left penniless and in desperate need for money. At the time, he was trying to build his Magnifying Transmitter at Wardenclyffe on Long Island, New York. The Magnifying Transmitter was a large tower that he originally told his backers was going to be the antenna for a worldwide radio system.

"Tesla was actually trying to build a system that could transmit electricity through the atmosphere so that you wouldn't have to rely on wires to bring power into your house or factory. All you would have to do is set up an antenna to draw power from the atmosphere. But before Tesla was able to finish his tower, Wall Street financier J. P. Morgan backed out of the deal. Tesla was left without any money and in great debt to a lot of people.

"So Perry was getting a lot headlines at the time, because of his attempt to reach the North

Pole. Tesla told his backers that he would show them what his Magnifying Transmitter was able to do. He was going to attempt to send a beam of energy from this transmitter to the North Pole. He could excite the ions in the upper atmosphere and create a huge light display. On the evening of June 30, 1908, with his associate George Schreff, Tesla went to Wardenclyffe Tower, which had been shut down for quite a while."

What happened next is the stuff of legend and rumor.

"Tesla focused the beam," Swartz continued, "and turned the transmitter on. And that was it, he thought. He received no reports that anything had happened at the North Pole. But within the next couple of days, news reports began to trickle in about the explosion over Tunguska. Tesla was pretty certain—he wasn't positive—but he was pretty certain that his Magnifying Transmitter had caused the explosion. To him, it just seemed too much of a coincidence that at the same time that he turned his transmitter on there was a gigantic explosion of some kind over Siberia.

"Some researchers have now calculated the path, and have demonstrated that Tunguska was within the line of sight, if you take into account the curvature over the North Pole, with Wardenclyffe, Long Island, and that Tesla must have overshot the North Pole. Which could be a good thing, because I don't think Tesla realized the amount of energy he was delivering.

"Instead of just creating an electrical charge to excite the atmosphere, kind of like a big neon tube, he actually created an explosion almost to the scale of the Hiroshima blast at the end of World War II."

But all things must pass.

"That was the last time," Swartz said, "that he was able to operate the Wardenclyffe Tower, because shortly thereafter he had to give away most of his assets to his creditors. In 1915 the tower was torn down and the land sold off. But that incident could actually have been the predecessor of what is now known as the modem Death Ray or particle beam weapons."

The Creation Of The Death Ray

From the Wardenclyffe Tower incident, Tesla moved on to further research and refine his deadly new invention, but he was not without competitors.

"The concept of the Death Ray was nothing

new back at the turn of the century," Swartz said. "There were a number of scientists working on the idea. I recently saw a photograph that showed British scientists in 1924 working on a Death Ray. There was no description, but it looked almost like they were working on a form of laser beam, which is very interesting. So it wasn't science fiction, it's just that the technology at the time wasn't up to the requirements to make a Death Ray feasible. There was no power source available to energize a beam to make it effective.

"But Tesla was probably one of the first scientists to come forward with something new in terms of actually building a Death Ray. In the mid1930s, Tesla laid out his preliminary design for accelerating microscopic particles of mercury and tungsten to incredible velocities. Tesla preferred that his beam be composed of a long train of single particles in order to minimize any scattering due to collisions within the beam.

"Electrostatic propulsion," Swartz continued, "of like charges would impart the necessary energy from the center of a highly charged sphere. These particles would then be squeezed forwards toward an opening and fly outward with a slingshot force of several million volts. What made Tesla's proposal different was that he could actually construct a mega-voltage device to make this possible."

Swartz explained why Tesla was succeeding where others hadn't.

"Tesla had long had the ability," he said, "to generate millions and millions of volts of electricity with his Tesla coil. So this was not an impossible feat for him. What was unique about his design was that he envisioned the inside of this Death Beam to be a vacuum, and the particles inside could then accelerate at a fantastic rate of speed. Then the idea would be to create a repulsive effect to shoot these particles out the other end at an incredible rate.

"Now at the time, achieving a vacuum inside a device was pretty near impossible. Tesla's idea was that he was going to use a highly concentrated stream of air right at the opening that would basically act as a plug. Then the air would be pumped out of the chamber and the process would be started. That's basically a layman's description of the Tesla Death Ray."

The Aftermath Of The Death Ray Invention

Like a great many of Tesla's inventions, the Death Ray never quite reached total fruition, in spite of its huge potential.

NIKOLA TESLA'S DEATH RAY AND THE
COLUMBIA SPACE SHUTTLE DISASTER

"It doesn't sound like much in description," Swartz said, "but apparently Tesla's Death Ray held a lot of promise, because at the time of his death, sll of Tesla's papers in his laboratory were seized by the United States government. There have been a number of FBI documents that have been released through the Freedom of Information Act that talked about the main interest that the United States government had in seizing Tesla's papers were for the design of his Death Ray."

Tesla had earlier made every effort to market his invention.

"Before that, when Tesla was still suffering financially, he tried to sell the designs of his Death Ray to various countries, including the United States and the Soviet Union, but no one seemed interested. Probably the main reason for that was that the United States and Britain were doing their own experiments with particle beam weapons. They probably felt that their own designs were superior.

"Well, this is a device that is not so easily built, as they found out," Swartz continued. "So when Tesla died, they confiscated all his papers in hopes of getting a better idea of what he was trying to develop. Then for some reason, and I've heard conflicting stories, most of his papers were then given back to the government of Yugoslavia. And a lot of researchers have speculated that the Soviet Union was then able to get hold of much of this information and were thus able to leap ahead of the U.S. in particle beam technology, all based on Tesla's original ideas."

Have Particle Beams Been Used Before?

The possibility that all that secret particle beam research might have surfaced from time to time is another factor in the Death Ray story.

"This information is highly classified," Swartz said, "and there have been a number of interesting events through the years that could be attributed to research in particle beam weaponry. We know this through a number of well-written articles in publications like Jane's Technology and Aviation Week & Space Technology.

Swartz gave the history of some happenings that raise a cloud of suspicion about the experimental use of Death Ray technology.

"One of the things that got the United States interested in the idea that the Soviet Union may have Tesla-based weaponry," he said, "was that in 1976, ham radio operators started reporting a strange radio signal coming over various frequencies on the short wave band. Ham radio operators all across the planet, but especially in the United States, were reporting this bizarre and very, very strong signal, which they later called 'the woodpecker,' because it would make like a drumming sound. It would just wash out everything else that was on or around that frequency.

"Apparently, this was a two-part experiment. Part of it was an over-the-horizon radar system that the Soviets were experimenting with so they could track missiles that would be flying over from the United States before they came over the horizon.

"On top of that, they were researching a particle beam weapon that would hone in, in conjunction with the woodpecker signal, to basically fry the electrical components of any kind of missile or plane coming over the horizon. There was actually a top-secret satellite photograph that shows this very interesting device in the Soviet Union that for all intents and purposes was a Tesla-based particle beam weapon."

There were even more similar events, according to Swartz.

"In the 1980s, there were a number of reports from airliners coming across the Pacific from Japan about anomalous clouds that were springing up over the Pacific, usually close to the extreme northeastern Soviet border. These clouds would just suddenly rear up out of nowhere, reached many miles up into the atmosphere, and estimated to be over 100 miles in diameter. Now it takes many hours for normal clouds to form, so when you see massive clouds suddenly exploding up beside you for no reason at all, the first thoughts were that these were nuclear explosions, nuclear tests, but there was no radiation associated with them. It was a sort of "cold explosion."

"One such incident occurred on April 9, 1984 when the Soviet Union tested a "cold explosion" off the coast of Japan, near the Kuril Islands. In the suddenly induced low pressure "cold zone" above the ocean, ocean water was sharply sucked up from the ocean, forming a dense cloud. Then air rushing into the low pressure zone forced the cloud upward, forming a mushroom much like that of an atomic explosion except for the absence of a flash and the absence of a shockwave moving out and away from the center of the explosion. As the cloud rises, it expands like a giant thunderhead buildup, except much faster. In this case the cloud rose to about 60,000 feet in about two minutes, spreading out until it reached a diameter of about 200 miles. The pilots and crews of several Boeing 747 jet airliners in the general vicinity saw the incident.

"Later it was determined that these were probably the results of what was called the 'Tesla Defense Dome' whereas a dome of highly charged particles over a given area would destroy any object entering into it. The energy would be pumped into the atmosphere using a Tesla Magnifying Transmitter. As long as the transmitter was operating, the dome would remain in place. Sort of like a glass bowl over a city, protecting it from planes or missiles. This would be a defensive weapon in that it wasn't a tight beam of energy locking on a plane to destroy it, but instead a passive device that is destructive only if you deliberately fly through it. Sort of the proverbial "line in the sand," except this would be a "line in the air."

Swartz also talked about an event that took place in 1974, this time near the Russian-Iranian border.

"This is a C.I.A. report, released under the Freedom of Information Act. The phenomenon was seen from two aircraft approaching Mehrabad Airport in Teheran, Iran on June 17, 1966 and reported by their pilots.

NIKOLA TESLA'S DEATH RAY AND THE
COLUMBIA SPACE SHUTTLE DISASTER

"On the far horizon deep within the Soviet Union, an intense spherical ball of light appeared, 'sitting on the horizon' so to speak. The globe of light increased to enormous size, dimming as it did so, literally filling an arc of the distant sky as it expanded. The sighting was shielded from most ground observers view at the airport itself due to an intervening mountain range that masked most of the phenomena from the ground. The silent, expanding globe was observed for four or five minutes before it faded away.

"There was also a report in the August 17 1980 edition of *The London Sunday Times* that contained a story accompanied with a sketch that detailed what could have been the testing of very large Tesla globes deep within the Soviet Union—the sightings were made in Afghanistan by British war cameraman Nick Downie. The phenomena seen were in the direction of the Saryshagan Missile Test Range, which-according to the U.S. Defense Departments Soviet Military Power 1986-contains one or more large directed energy weapons (DEW's)."

Has the technology from these early experimental versions of the Death Ray moved on to heights we can only imagine? Have we seen just the tip of the iceberg of what has been created offstage by governments and scientists determined to make the seemingly impossible a terrifying reality? It may be quite a long time before we, the public, learn just what lengths particle beam research has reached.

Chapter Five

The Trail Leads To Columbia

The interview with Tim Swartz continued, with Swartz telling the story of the Death Ray and the many stages of its development leading up to the terrible, terrible morning of February 1, 2003.

Just How Much Secrecy Is At Work Here?

So what we're dealing with are scientists who basically picked up the ball from Tesla and ran with it?

"Yeah," Swartz replied. "You know, after World War 11, both the United States and the Soviet Union were in a Cold War. They were developing missiles and atomic weapons and they were also trying to come up with anything else that could give them an edge over the other. The whole idea originally of the Tesla-based energy weapons was that they were to be used as a missile defense shield that could knock missiles or planes out of the sky before they had a chance to explode over your territory. So both the United

NIKOLA TESLA'S DEATH RAY AND THE COLUMBIA SPACE SHUTTLE DISASTER

States and the Soviet Union and probably other countries—China, maybe even Israel—were working on these same devices.

"Now, whether or not they're currently very effective is still open to conjecture," Swartz said. "It's my opinion that if these Tesla-based energy weapons, at least currently, were that effective, we would be seeing them used more often and not being kept secret. If somebody really had a controllable particle beam energy weapon, based on Tesla technology, I think they would be all too happy to let the rest of the world know that they've got this weapon. It's still speculation on just how controllable these weapons really are.

"The science is there," he continued. "Everyone has known for years that it can be done. It's just a matter of, 'Is our technology up to it currently?' It wasn't in Tesla's time. If we look at the Wardenclyffe-Tunguska connection, it definitely wasn't controllable. Tesla obviously didn't have a proper way to aim something like this. And now, since we've had more experience with things like laser beams, which are easy enough to aim now, particle beam weapons could be just as effective. But the beam is so concentrated—think of a laser beam in concentration, but instead of amplified light, you have microscopic particles, highly charged and ionized, blasting in a concentrated beam with millions of volts of electricity energizing them. That's a pretty awesome thing-"

But What If The Secrecy Is For Real?

Swartz acknowledged, on the other hand, that the rumored secrecy around the Tesla Death Ray might in fact be all too real.

"One of the reasons you would want to keep it secret is that that's your ace," he reasoned. "You're going to keep that hidden until the very last minute. And you're not going to use it unless you really, really have to. And then, when you really have to, you strike your enemy down. Boom! 'Don't mess with us. We've got this!' So if there was a reason to keep something like this secret, that alone would be it. Because, what's the saying? 'Nobody is more dangerous than when you think they're at their weakest.'

"But again, I think probably one of the major reasons that this technology is being kept secret is that it's not an easy technology to control. You could just as easily kill yourself in operating something like this as too kill someone else."

Did HAARP Bring Down Columbia?

Now the conversation moved on to the heart

of the matter: the Columbia disaster.

Swartz began to tell the tale of an amateur radio operator who monitors the HAARP transmissions out of Alaska.

"A radio operator by the name of Marshall Smith has reported that on the day that Columbia was coming down, HAARP was doing what he called their 'missile defense radio transmissions.' Now, a lot of researchers have asserted that the HAARP facility in Alaska is the U.S. version of a Tesla electromagnetic energy weapon, albeit more sophisticated than the ones that the Soviet Union was working on, and going quite a ways beyond Tesla's original concepts.

"HAARP allegedly takes this idea one step further," Swartz continued, "and uses different frequencies of electromagnetic energy, radio frequency, to achieve the same effects. So you transmit your energy into the atmosphere, focus it at a distance, which then enables it to be aimed anywhere on the globe. Now some people have speculated that the HAARP facility, at least in part, is a missile defense installation, or at least an experimental missile defense installation, using radio frequencies, to try to knock missiles out of the sky.

NIKOLA TESLA'S DEATH RAY AND THE COLUMBIA SPACE SHUTTLE DISASTER

"For several years, beginning about 1998, HAARP is normally turned on during the summer months, starting several hours before midnight. They are doing atmospheric auroral zone research for several hours each night when the sky is very dark, during that part of the month when the bright moon is below the horizon. That is the "University Research" mode. The shortwave transmitter pulses may have both long and short pulses with about equal-length spaces in between, and the pulse lengths may vary, depending on the academic research experiment, from three to 30 seconds.

"Following the 9-11 World Trade Center attack, and just minutes after the President declared the highest Defense Condition Four (DefCon4), HAARP began transmitting at highest power for 18 hours in 'deep-sea communication' mode. This is the only way to communicate the DefCon4 condition and updated battle commands to the US nuclear submarines on station miles deep in the ocean.

The 'Air Force Missile Defense Shield' mode is usually heard as four or five second pulses about 20 seconds apart. The pulses also are modulated with circular polarization, changing in tone slightly faster or slower than the one Hz base frequency. This causes very fast relativistic electrons or ions to be sprayed into outer space arcing from north to south magnetic pole, from the ionosphere, either upward to the magneto-sphere, or downward from the magnetosphere to the ionosphere.

"These particles, moving at nearly the speed of light, stay only in the vacuum of space and are stopped whenever they hit the atmosphere. The focused fast moving particles can penetrate and damage the electronics of an incoming nuclear missile warhead and cause the missile to spin out of control and burn up as it re-enters the earth's atmosphere.

"The damage effect is similar to the strong radiation from a nearby nuclear explosion. Thus the 'missile shield' mode can quickly destroy incoming missiles almost anywhere in the world even before they re-enter the atmosphere. The graduate student technical research reports on the HAARP website for the summer study programs of 1999 and 2000 reveal they have succeeded in producing particle flow along 'certain magnetic field lines.' This is a secretive or obtuse way of saying that they have finally implemented a 'focused missile defense shield' mode.

But back to the story of Marshall Smith.

NIKOLA TESLA'S DEATH RAY AND THE
COLUMBIA SPACE SHUTTLE DISASTER

"So now Marshall Smith, who is a licensed commercial radio engineer since the 1960's, reported that on the morning of Saturday Feb 1, 2003, HAARP was transmitting from 4:15 AM to about 7:20 AM PST in missile defense mode. That was the first HAARP transmission since late 2002. Columbia reentered the atmosphere over California at 5:53 AM PST, right in the middle of HAARP's transmissions. Smith speculates that this may have been an accidental testing—or maybe deliberate, though I'd hate to think that—but an accidental testing of HAARP's antimissile defense capabilities. The space shuttle accidentally got in the way and was brought down. I find it very interesting that the same radio frequencies that Tesla talked about using for his electromagnetic defense shield are the same frequencies that HAARP was broadcasting on the morning that the shuttle came down."

Who Is To Blame?

Swartz next asked a very difficult question.

"Was it deliberate? Was it an accident? It's really hard to say. I would like to think that it was an accident, but we'll never know. Nobody's going to come forward and say, 'Oh by the way, we accidentally killed seven astronauts because somebody left the transmitter in Alaska on a little too long.' But if that's the case, it also shows how effective this Tesla-based technology can be over great distances.

"It would be interesting to see just exactly where the Columbia started to break up as it was coming in over the Pacific, whether or not it was in alignment with where HAARP was broadcasting. Columbia could have entered into an invisible cloud of extremely high energy radiation spewing southward from Gakona, Alaska.

"The cloud of relativistic electrons may have penetrated deeply into Columbia, instantly causing strange heating on the northern or left side of the spacecraft toward Alaska, both on the left wing and even on the upper left side of the craft near the left cargo bay door. Because the radiation cloud is coming from the northern side, not from below, only the left side of Columbia was seriously affected at first. But as the energy continued to work on the structure of the ship, it eventually led to a complete break up.

There were similar concerns when Flight 800 went down over the East Coast, Swartz said.

"The same night that Flight 800 went down, HAARP was transmitting across various frequencies, not just one frequency, but across a number of frequencies, and using a lot of power, as well. Nobody really knows just exactly what they were trying to achieve with those experiments, but it always seems that whenever HAARP is fired up, there is an increased potential for airline disasters across the planet. However, we can't just blame HAARP for everything; there are other, similar transmitters operating in secret by other countries, so international terrorism is a possibility."

Could It Have Been Deliberate?

The interview next broached the unthinkable. What if the Columbia had been shot down intentionally?

"Now we're getting into all kinds of dangerous thoughts, like political conspiracies," Swartz answered. "But to do something like that, you're dealing with a weapon of terror. That's pretty frightening. Right now, at this very moment, with the United States, in its somewhat belligerent stance toward the rest of the world, a particle beam weapon that can be aimed to hit anywhere at any time, with devastating effects that can't be traced, I think would really make the world community sit up and take notice.

"And I would think that with the current state

of world affairs we should pay close attention to unexplained accidents and explosions, because we may be seeing the start of an energy beam brinkmanship going on with various countries who may have this kind of technology. So it's really hard to say, but something like energy beam weapons would be excellent terror weapons, because you just never know when it's coming. There's no warning, and it can't be traced either."

The Unknown Photographer

The unidentified photographer mentioned earlier also caught the interest of Swartz, who gave his own perspective on what may be the only real evidence of a Death Ray being involved in the shuttle disaster.

"The morning that the shuttle was coming down," Swartz said, "there was an amateur astronomer who was out taking photographs as the shuttle crossed Northern California. This was a man who had a lot of experience taking these kinds of pictures. Afterwards, he noticed on his film some unusual light patterns that seemed to show a corkscrewing light that followed the shuttle's plasma trail, which is the trail that comes off behind the shuttle as it drops down through the atmosphere.

NIKOLA TESLA'S DEATH RAY AND THE
COLUMBIA SPACE SHUTTLE DISASTER

"The corkscrewing light was purple in color, a different shade than the plasma trail coming off the shuttle. It went past the shuttle and then made a sharp right angle turn and then went back into the shuttle. At this time, none of these photographs have been released to the public. NASA immediately took them and little has been heard about them since.

"Now an astronaut who personally came and took the photographs back to NASA, called the photographs just incredible. She had never seen anything like them before. The astronaut's name is Tammy Jernigan. She said, 'Wow.' The photo in question is just one of five that was captured by the astronomer, and obviously it was unusual enough, based on his previous experience, that he felt he should report it."

Tesla's Death Ray Could Have Done It

"What's interesting about this," Swartz explained, "is that according to Nikola Tesla's original research with his energy beam weapon, he could make a beam of energy that would follow an ionized path to a source. Now to take that a step back, you could take an energy weapon and beam it into the atmosphere. It would then find an ionized trail of plasma and follow it to its source, and then empty out all of its energy at that source.

"Somehow,, somebody could feasibly shoot an energy beam weapon into the atmosphere, and it would home in onto the shuttle's plasma trail as the shuttle heats up as it enters the atmosphere. It would then follow that trail to the shuttle and cause it to explode."

Are Terrorists Behind It All?

"Whether it was by accident or if it was a form of terrorism, we'll never know," Swartz said. "The United States government is never going to come forward and say terrorists knocked our shuttle out of the sky. They would never admit it.

"And there is some good evidence that people other than those associated with the military have been experimenting with Tesla-based energy systems. The Japanese cult, Aum Supreme Truth also employed a number of ex-Soviet scientists at a research lab in Australia. In the area surrounding that lab there were numerous reports of loud explosions, fireballs rushing across the sky, actual seismic events. It looks now that they were actually doing research into Tesla energy weapons.

"It's a frightening thought " Swartz concluded, "to consider that you've got countries aiming deadly weapons at each other. It's another thing to think that a terrorist organization like Al Qaida could get hold of something like this. I mean, just think of the devastation that could happen if something like this got into the wrong hands. It's very **'James Bondian.'"**

TESLA'S DEATH RAY

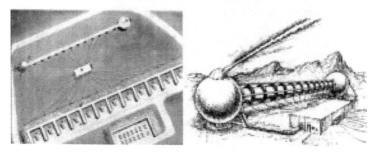

A Soviet facility seen from an orbiting atellite (left), and the device that projects the destructive beam (artist's rendering right).

NIKOLA TESLA'S DEATH RAY AND THE COLUMBIA SPACE SHUTTLE DISASTER

Declassified FBI documents reveal that one of the main reasons for the government's interest and eventual seizure of Tesla's belongings was because of his Death Ray. Truckloads of his notes and research papers were later sent to Wright-Patterson Air Force Base where it is thought that early developments of the U.S. Death Ray began.

NIKOLA TESLA'S DEATH RAY AND THE
COLUMBIA SPACE SHUTTLE DISASTER

Mr. Clarence Kelly
Director
F.B.I.
Washington, DC

ALL INFORMATION CONTAINED
HEREIN IS UNCLASSIFIED
DATE 2-5-12 BY

Dear Mr. Kelly:

Mr. Allen and Mr. Ruchlehaus, former acting Director of the FBI, contacted me in 1973 regarding the unavailability of American microfilm records of Nikola Tesla's unpublished diary (now in the Belgrade museum, arranged by month per folder).

At the time I discounted the possibility that these unpublished discoveries had military significance. But because of experiments now under way at Hill AFB, I now suspect such military applications exist and feel it imperative that you be notified, particularly in view of the fact that the Soviets have primary access to the entire collection.

In 1945, we talked to a Private Bloyce Fitzgerald, who stated he had been associated with Tesla, and that the Army believed that Tesla's "death ray" is the only defense against atom bombs.

It was very clear we had no responsibility for Tesla's effects, that the Alien Property Custodian seized them and as learned later that Naval authorities made microfilms of all his papers.

Kosanovich communicated with the Bureau on March 29, 1950, and under date of April 3, 1950, in response to his request for the microfilms of the papers of Tesla, who was a relative of Kosanovich, we advised Kosanovich that this Bureau had never been in possession of Tesla's papers.

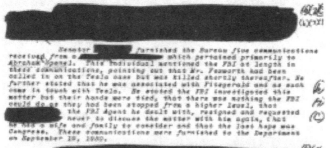

Senator ____ furnished the Bureau five communications received from a ____ which pertained primarily to Abraham Spanel. This individual mentioned the FBI at length in these communications, pointing out that Mr. Foxworth had been called in on the Tesla case but was killed shortly thereafter. He further stated that he was associated with Fitzgerald and as such came in touch with Tesla. He stated the FBI investigated this matter but their hands were tied, that there was nothing the FBI could do as they had been stopped from a higher level, that ____ the FBI Agent he dealt with, resigned and requested never to discuss the matter with him again, that he had a wife and family to consider and that the last hope was Congress. These communications were furnished to the Department on September 19, 1980.

59

NIKOLA TESLA'S DEATH RAY AND THE COLUMBIA SPACE SHUTTLE DISASTER

Nikola Tesla shown with his Magnifying Transmitter producing "Teleforce" with "rays of energy many thousands of horsepower that can be transmitted by a stream thinner than a hair, so that nothing can resist."

Chapter Six

Secret NASA Transmissions

And The Alien Presence

Along with the fact that a Tesla-based Death Ray may have brought down the Columbia, another possibility also presents itself. Could the UFOs of varying size and description often reported by both astronauts and cosmonauts be the true culprits here?

Are the many video transmissions, which clearly show that our shuttle crews are not alone out there, evidence of an alien presence that is closely watching our space program and intervening where it deems necessary? A video called *The Secret NASA Transmissions: 'The Smoking Gun,'* issued by a Venice, California, company called UFO Central Home Video, makes quite a convincing case for that possibility.

The Stage Is Set

The video begins, dramatically enough, with these words: "Since the dawn of time, man has cast an envious eye towards the heavens, and speculated about what it may contain. And for the past half-century, he has conducted an exhaustive yet still fruitless search for the telltale signature of extraterrestrial life.

"But in the summer of 1999, a cable TV station in Vancouver, Canada, emerged from the shadows to lay claim to such a discovery. This video forms part of an ongoing and coordinated effort to ensure full public disclosure."

Next we see old news film of former President Ronald Reagan's address to the United Nations in 1983, which is now popularly known as "The Little Green Man Speech." After outlining how an alien threat from off the planet would immediately unite all the warring countries on Earth, Reagan surprised everyone by posing the question, "Is not an alien force already among us?"

The Search For Extraterrestrial Intelligence (SETI) is discussed, and is regarded by the video's authors as a failure in its attempt to uncover an alien presence by sifting through hundreds of billions of radio signals. The jury is still out on SETI, of course, but many skeptics continue to regard it as a complete waste of time, money and resources.

NIKOLA TESLA'S DEATH RAY AND THE
COLUMBIA SPACE SHUTTLE DISASTER

Meanwhile, the video tells us that there is a law against NASA doing the same thing.

"It is a curious fact," the British-accented narrator intones, "that NASA is forbidden by Congress to spend time or money to seek out communications, signals or any form of contact with an extraterrestrial intelligence. But what if an extraterrestrial intelligence was to seek out contact with NASA, either directly or indirectly?"

It is that question which the video gamely tries to deal with, enlisting the help of one Martyn Stubbs.

Martyn Stubbs And His One-Man Crusade

Martyn Stubbs is the manager of a local cable public access station in Vancouver, Canada. In the summer of 1999, he contacted Graham Birdsall, the editor of the British UFO Magazine and spoke to him by phone for forty-five minutes. Stubbs proceeded to recount an extraordinary story in which he claimed to have accessed NASA transmissions from numerous space shuttle missions that stretched back over a period of several years.

Amidst all of this footage, over 2,500 hours worth, Stubbs claimed to have stumbled on to palpable evidence for the reality of not one, but two, forms of extraterrestrial spacecraft.

The first type of UFO observed is a spherical ball of light, which has turned up repeatedly since the space program's earliest beginnings. In the early 1960s, Astronaut John Glenn reported them as resembling "fireflies," and NASA at the time even publicly stated they might be "living critters." There is a great deal of video evidence to support that claim, even though NASA's public spokesman has denied it with a vengeance.

The type of UFO that Stubbs discovered looks on tape like a rodshaped, self-illurninated bar of light. It is only possible to actually see the UFO when the video is broken down frame-by-frame. Using his skills as a videotape editor, Stubbs looked at the video and saw that the UFO was traveling so quickly that it only showed up in a few of the frames. There were 60 individual frames per one second of tape, meaning the object was moving out of sight in a tiny fraction of a second of what is called "real time."

Stubbs said he took his videotape discovery to the scientific community, including a Professor Weinberg, from Simon Frazier University in Canada. The scientists seemed at first to only humor Stubbs. When they actually saw the evidence with their own eyes, however, their interest led them to do further tests themselves.

"It blew the scientists minds!" Stubb exclaims. "They realized that the object had to actually be there and that it couldn't be faked."

At the urging of Professor Weinberg, Stubbs attempted to further test the reality of what was showing up on video by seeing if the same phenomenon would be found on somebody else's tapes as well. So Stubbs recorded CNN's live feed of a shuttle mission, and subjected it to the same frame-by-frame analysis.

"There they were again," Stubbs said. "How much more proof do you need? I didn't want to come forth until I was certain, and now I am."

Interestingly, Stubbs is not one to cry "Cover-Up!"

"The Canadian Space Agency has been very cooperative," he said, "and places like JPL have been willing to look at the evidence. No one's threatening us and there haven't been any agents at my door."

But even as NASA officially continues to deny that anything remotely like intelligently controlled extraterrestrial spacecraft are responsible for the strange images on the shuttle mission videotapes, many astronauts and cosmonauts continue to publicly state their belief that they have personally seen things out in space that seem to be genuine alien phenomena. As the videos cover amusingly boasts, this is "the most popular underground tape among astronauts."

The Frightening Implications

With their proven ability to flit in and out sight around our spacecraft, can we logically ask if the alien presence on Earth and in the heavens above can be responsible for things like the Columbia and Challenger disasters?

Or, is the phenomena documented by Stubbs an example of the manmade ball lightning discussed earlier in this book by Tim Swartz? Do scientists on Earth have the ability to project Death Ray technology far out into space, where NASA cameras inadvertently record them?

Either scenario is a scary one, to be sure.

Is A Death Ray Already Out There?

While Stubbs primarily argues for the extraterrestrial hypothesis regarding the anomalous phenomena showing up on all those thousands of hours of tape, it is worth noting that there may be alternate explanations for some of them. For example, the video shows a tape of NASA observing the Russian space station MIR when a couple of spherical objects fly by.

The woman on the NASA microphone dryly comments that there are "shooting stars" appearing in the shot, but then the shooting stars suddenly change direction, looking unmistakably to be intelligently guided and controlled. No comment is made as the shooting stars disappear from view. A Death Ray tracking its prey?

Still another tape depicts an object, perhaps a beam of some sort, that shoots up from the Earth and then appears similarly to change direction suddenly and move quickly out of the camera's range. Was it a particle beam locked onto its target with unheard of tenacity?

The video also recounts the story of a Russian cosmonaut who was in Sao Paulo, Brazil, to lecture at a UFO convention a few years ago. He was asked if there are Star Wars weapons out there in space already that could account for some of these phenomena. The cosmonaut replied that yes, it was generally understood that such weapons were now in place and that their existence is taken for granted.

Is Star Wars the latest version of the particle

beam weapon first envisioned by Nikola Tesla? Did the great inventor set in motion a chain of events that led ultimately to the destruction of the space shuttle Columbia? This book has attempted to piece together some answers based on the available information, but we are a long way from knowing the complete truth.

NOTE: THE SECRET NASA TRANSMISSIONS video is available for $29.95 plus $5.00 shipping from Global Communications, PO Box 753, New Brunswick, NJ 08903

This is a still taken from a video camera on space shuttle mission STS 48. The image seems to show strange UFOs in orbit and what appears to be a beam of high energy being shot from the Earths surface by a particle beam weapon. Second is an artist's rendition of how this event may have looked.

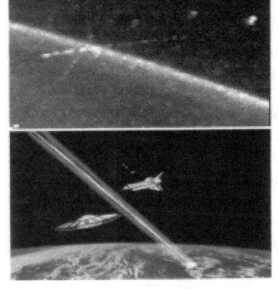

Chapter Seven

Top-Secret Research of Death Rays

Any child who watches cartoons on television is familiar with the concept of a "ray gun." Science fiction stories from, the beginning were filled with tales of ray guns and beam weapons used not only by alien invaders but also by futuristic heroes such as Flash Gordon or Buck Rogers. This has continued to modern times in movies and TV shows such as Star Trek with their laser and phaser guns.

What few people realize is that these "science fiction" ray guns are based on historical fact as scientists have sought for a long time to develop a functional ray gun, or Death Ray, that is inexpensive, easy to operate and transport.

World War I, it is thought, served as a catalyst for the development of what was considered at the time as more "humane" weapons. Although the United States did not enter World War I until 1917, Americans were horrified by the carnage on the western front. The opposing armies, huddled in elaborate networks of trenches, had fought to an early but bloody stalemate. The problem was that entrenched troops, equipped with the recently perfected machine gun, were virtually invincible. They could easily mow down enemy soldiers who attacked.

American inventors offered visionary solutions to break the stalemate on the western front. The first wave of visionary weapon popular in the World War I years relied on electricity for effectiveness instead of size. By harnessing the seemingly magical power of this new force, some enthusiasts believed they could create the ultimate weapon.

In 1918 Hugo Gernsback, known as a publisher, radio experimenter, and later as the founder of the first science fiction magazine, offered the idea of an automatic soldier to be built of "shell-proof Tungsten steel" and powered by electricity. He envisioned dozens of these automatons replacing human soldiers in the forward line of trenches firing on the enemy according to directions received by radio.

The most spectacular of the proposed applications of electricity was the Death Ray, a concentrated beam of electricity that could destroy people, vehicles, or structures. H.G. Wells is usually credited with first imagining the death ray, wielded by the invading Martians in his 1898 novel *War of the Worlds*, and may have been inspired by the discovery of X-rays a few years earlier.

The Search For A New Weapon

In the spring of 1924 newspapers worldwide carried a series of fascinating articles about Death Rays and their inventors. Harry Grindell-Matthews of London lead the contenders in this early race. *The New York Times* of May 21st had this report:

Paris, May 20 - If confidence of Grindell Matthews, inventor of the so-called 'diabolical ray,' in his discovery is justified it may become possible to put the whole of an enemy army out of action, destroy any force of airplanes attacking a city or paralyze any fleet venturing within a certain distance of the coast by invisible rays. So much the inventor consented to tell *The New York Times* correspondent today while continuing to refuse to divulge the exact nature of the rays beyond that they are used to direct an electric current able to perform the program just mentioned.

Grindell-Matthews stated that his destructive

rays would operate over a distance of four miles and that the maximum distance for this type of weapon would be seven or eight miles. Asked if it would be possible to destroy an approaching enemy fleet, the inventor said it would not, because "Ships, like land, are in continual contact with the earth, but what I can do is to put the ships out of action by the destruction of vital parts of the machinery, and also by putting the crews temporarily out of action through shock." Airplanes, on the other hand, could be completely destroyed. As soon as his ray touched the plane it would burst into flames and fall to earth. Grindell-Matthews asserted, "I am convinced the Germans possess the ray." He believed, though, they were carrying out their experiments with high frequencies and at high power, around 200 kilowatts, and could not control the weapon to hit a specific target. So far, said Grindell-Matthews, he had tried tests at 500 watts in his laboratory over a distance of sixty-four feet.

A French company, the Great Rhone Engineering Works of Lyon, had offered Grindell-Matthews extensive financial backing that would allow him to test his device at much higher power levels. He replied that would not undertake such tests "except under conditions of absolute safety on a wide tract of uninhabited land," such was the destructive power of his rays.

Details of the "diabolical rays'" destructive power surfaced that August. "Tests have been reported where the ray has been used to stop the operation of automobiles by arresting the action of the magnetos, and an quantity of gunpowder is said to have been exploded by playing the beams on it from a distance of thirty-six feet." Grindell-Matthews was able, also, to electrocute mice, shrivel plants, and light the wick of an oil lamp from the same distance away.

His own laboratory assistants themselves became unintentional victims of the ray. When crossing its path during tests they were either knocked unconscious by violent electrical shocks or received intense burns. The inventor stated that, although it would be possible to kill enemy infantry with the ray, "It would be quite easy to graduate the electric power used so that hostile troops would only be knocked out long enough to effect their capture. "

Who Was Grindell-Matthews?

By any standard Harry Grindell-Matthews was all that an eccentric scientist should be. Working in a remote laboratory in the Welsh mountains he claimed to have invented, among other things, an electronic beam that earned him the nickname "Death Ray."

Born in 1880, Grindell-Matthews was educated at Bristol Merchant Venturers' College (England) and at nineteen volunteered for the Boer War, in which he was twice wounded. Trained as a research scientist, specializing in electricity, he was intrigued by the possibilities of radio telephony, then in its infancy, and as early as 1911, from Ely racecourse, Cardiff, he succeeded in conversing with the airman B. C. Hucks in a plane two miles away and traveling at high speed.

Grindell-Matthews, like many other inventors before and since, often failed to develop his ideas commercially. As soon as he had successfully solved a particular problem, his mind would leap ahead with a fresh idea.

Following the onset of World War I his experiments in developing a robot boat controlled by a light beam, using a new light-sensitive material, selenium, brought him quickly to the attention of the British Government. He proved his claims in trials at Portsmouth, using a larger steamship that was controlled by a naval searchlight more than five miles away.

The Government coughed up a first instalment

of £25,000 on the proviso that Grindell-Matthews could further develop his device and produce an aerial torpedo as an answer to the Zeppelin — but no more seems to have been heard of the idea. After the war his probing mind went off in yet another direction — the problem of talking film and in 1921 the inventor made a talkie of Sir Ernest Shackleton delivering his farewell speech before setting off for Antarctica.

In 1924 Grindell-Matthews really set the world a-buzz when newspapers got hold of the rumor that he had invented an invisible ray which would, as one report put it: "Stop a motor working, kill plant life, destroy vermin, explode gunpowder, fire cartridges and light lamps."

Inevitably, invention and inventor were dubbed Death Ray and the man himself quickly became the center of fantastic public interest. Although he himself said: "I knew I had at present little more than an interesting peashooter', the public wanted to believe that he had the ability to control armies, to make aircraft fall from the sky, in effect, the power to stop war."

It was the suggestion that the new device could cut out aircraft engines in flight that caused the Air Ministry to request an official test. Grindell-Matthews happily obliged, but the men from the Ministry were unimpressed, stating that all the inventor had demonstrated was that he could stop at will a small motorcycle engine from some fifteen yards, no mean feat as it happens. Nevertheless, they were prepared to offer him £1,000 against further tests, on a petrol engine that was to be provided by the Government.

The inventor declined however and announced shortly after that he was heading off the France, a Lyons company having made a 'princely offer' for his secret, which he now claimed could kill or disable men at a distance of four miles. He did fly to France but meanwhile his associates obtained a High Court injunction, preventing him selling the device.

Questions were asked in the House of Commons and one skeptical MP enquired whether it was true that a Ministry official had placed himself within ten yards of the ray, which was supposed to kill at a distance of several miles. A Government spokesman replied that it was true and added that the official was doing well.

Whatever the truth about the ray's lethal properties, in July 1924, Grindell-Matthews announced he had lost the sight of his left eye as a result of his experiments. In that month he arrived in New York, thoroughly disgusted with the neglect he had suffered in Britain and doubts cast upon the validity of his experimental work. The following March he returned briefly to England to announce he had sold his death ray to the United States and was going to settle in that country.

No more was heard of the remarkable Welsh inventor until Christmas Eve, 1930, when late shoppers in the Hampstead Heath area of London were startled to see a beam of light shoot up about 6,000 feet into the cloud base. For several minutes the light continued to play back and forth on the cloud when suddenly it took on the form of a rather voluptuous 'angel' with outstretched wings gliding across the sky. Traffic stopped and crowds gathered to gaze in awe at the sight. The angel vanished shortly after, only to be replaced by the words, *A Happy Christmas*. Grindell-Matthews was back.

He had been operating his latest invention from a pair of film location trucks and had already demonstrated his 'sky projector' in New York, by throwing a picture of the Stars and Stripes and the American eagle onto the clouds.

"The advantages of the machine in war time for conveying coded messages to airmen are obvious," he pointed out. "It also has many possibilities, for example, for electioneering purposes, for advertising, and also for announcing important items of news."

Other demonstrations followed, including a huge glowing clock showing the correct time in the sky at Blackheath. But the sky projector proved to be yet another fifteen minute wonder and, once again, Grindell-Matthews was to drop out of the limelight.

He re-emerged five years later giving newspaper interviews from a bungalow laboratory 1,500 feet up on Tor Cloud, a barren mountain in South Wales. Reporters told their readers how they, exclusively, had penetrated the ring of armed guards, barbed wire fences and secret-eye burglar alarms around the hideout, to learn how the inventor of the death-ray now planned to defend London against any foreign attack.

This was to be accomplished by firing rockets to a height of 30,000 feet where, at that altitude, aerial torpedoes would release a brood of bombs suspended from parachutes by 500 feet of wire. Just how this was to be achieved is another matter but in July 1935, "only a certain amount of experimental work remained to be done" and "foreign governments, as well as the British, are eager for news of his work," it was reported.

Two years later, in addition to his air defense scheme Grindell-Matthews was reportedly perfecting apparatus that would detect submarines thirty miles away. By 1939 he was "only seeking new and more vital propellants" for his rockets. But by the time he died, aged sixty-one, during September 1941, in Clydach, Glamorgan, German bombers had repeatedly attacked London and other cities without any apparent hindrance from invisible rays or bombs suspended from skyhooks.

The inventor's personal life was shrouded in as much mystery as his work. In January 1938, he became the fifth husband of Madam Ganna Walska, a wealthy Polish opera singer of whom one unkind critic wrote: "better seen than heard." The newspapers referred to Madam Walksa as the "£25,000,000 bride" because of the fortunes of her four previous husbands.

While the evidence to back Grindell-Matthews' claims for his death ray and aerial torpedoes never really surfaced he was still an exceptional inventor. Talking films and such minor inventions as electronic burglar alarms and automatic street lighting can be attributed to his work.

NIKOLA TESLA'S DEATH RAY AND THE COLUMBIA SPACE SHUTTLE DISASTER

A national newspaper after his death carried this simple notice: "An electrical research worker who claimed to have invented a Death Ray, Mr Harry Grindell-Matthews, has left £522."

More Death Rays Surface

On May 25th, another Death Ray was announced in England. Doctor T. F. Wall, a lecturer in electrical research in Sheffield University, applied for a patent for means of transmitting electrical energy in any direction without the use of wires. According to one report even though he has not made tests on a large scale yet: "Dr. Wall expressed the belief that his invention would be capable of destroying life, stopping airplanes in flight and bringing motor cars to a standstill." On a more positive note, he added that his invention would have beneficial applications in surgical and medical operations.

Germany joined the technology race on May 25th when it announced its electrical weapon. As the *Chicago Tribune* reported: "That the German Government has an invention of death rays that will bring down airplanes, halt tanks on the battlefields, ruin automobile motors, and spread a curtain of death like the gas clouds of the recent war was the information given to Reichstag members by Herr Wulle, chief of the militarists in that body. It is learned that three inventions have been perfected in Germany for the same purpose and have been patented."

Sensing something of importance the **New York Times** copyrighted its story of May 28th on a ray weapon developed by the Soviets. The story opened: "News has leaked out from the Communist circles in Moscow that behind Trotsky's recent war-like utterance lies an electromagnetic invention, by a Russian engineer named Grammachikoff, for destroying airplanes."

Tests of the destructive ray, the *Times* continued, had begun the previous August with the aid of German technical experts. A large-scale demonstration at Podosinsky Aerodome near Moscow was so successful that the revolutionary Military Council and the Political Bureau decided to fund enough electronic anti-aircraft stations to protect sensitive areas of Russia. Similar, but more powerful, stations were to be constructed to disable the electrical mechanisms of warships. The Commander of the Soviet Air Services, Rosenholtz, was so overwhelmed by the ray weapon demonstration that he proposed "to curtail the activity of the air fleet, because the invention rendered a large air fleet unnecessary for the purpose of defense."

An English engineer, J. H. Hamil, offered the American army plans for producing " an invisible ray capable of stopping airplanes and automobiles in mid-flight," invented by a German scientist. The ray device was reportedly used the previous summer to bring down French planes over Bavaria.

Hamil noted, however, "the fundamental work was done by Nikola Tesla in Colorado Springs about 30 years ago. He built a powerful electrical coil. It was found that the dynamos and other electrical apparatus of a Colorado fuel company within 100 yards or so were all put out of business.

Hamil believed the Tesla coil scattered rays which short-circuited electrical machinery at close range. Laboratories all over the world, he added, were testing methods of stepping up the Tesla coil to produce its effects at greater distances. "Working on an entirely different principle," Hamil said, "the German scientist has succeeded in projecting and directing electrical power."

Next, *The Colorado Springs Gazette* ran a local interest item on May 30 with the headline:

NIKOLA TESLA'S DEATH RAY AND THE
COLUMBIA SPACE SHUTTLE DISASTER

Tesla Discovered Death Ray in Experiments He Made Here. The story recounted, with a feeling of local pride, the inventor's 1899 researches financed by John Jacob Astor. Tesla's Colorado Springs tests were well remembered by local residents. With a 200-foot pole topped by a large copper sphere rising above his laboratory he generated potentials that discharged lightning bolts up to 135 feet long.

Thunder from the released energy could be heard 15 miles away in Cripple Creek. People walking along the streets were amazed to see sparks jumping between their feet and the ground, and flames of electricity would spring from a tap when anyone turned them on for a drink of water. Light bulbs within 100 feet of the experimental tower glowed when they were turned off. Horses at the livery stable received shocks through their metal shoes and bolted from the stalls. Even insects were affected: Butterflies became electrified and "helplessly swirled in circles, their wings spouting blue halos of 'St. Elmo's Fire."

According to Oliver Nichelson in his 1989 article: *Nikola Tesla's Long Range Weapon*, the most pronounced effect, and the one that captured the attention of death ray inventors, occurred at the

Colorado Springs Electric Company generating station.

One day while Tesla was conducting a high power test, the crackling from inside the laboratory suddenly stopped. Bursting into the lab Tesla demanded to know why his assistant had disconnected the coil. The assistant protested that had not done anything. The power from the city's generator, the assistant said, must have quit. When the angry Tesla telephoned the power company he received an equally angry reply that the electric company had not cut the power, but that Tesla's experiment had destroyed the generator.

The inventor explained to **The Electrical Experimenter**, in August of 1917 what had occurred that fateful day. While running his transmitter at a power level of "several hundred kilowatts" high frequency currents were set up in the electric company's generators. These powerful currents "caused heavy sparks to jump thru the winds and destroy the, insulation." When the insulation failed, the generator shorted out and was destroyed.

Some years later, 1935, he elaborated on the destructive potential of his transmitter in the February issue of **Liberty** magazine: "My invention requires a large plant, but once it is established it will be possible to destroy anything, men or machines, approaching within a radius of 200 to 250 miles."

He went on to make a distinction between his invention and those brought forward by others. He claimed that his device did not use any so-called "radiations" because such radiation cannot be produced in large amounts and rapidly becomes weaker over distance.

It is supposed that Tesla likely had in mind a Grindell-Matthews type of device which, according to contemporary reports, used a powerful ultraviolet beam to make the air conducting so that high energy current could be directed to the target.

The range of an ultraviolet searchlight would be much less than what Tesla was claiming. As he put it: "all the energy of New York City (approximately two million horsepower [1.5 billion watts]) transformed into rays and projected twenty miles, would not kill a human being." On the contrary, he said: "My apparatus projects particles which may be relatively large or of microscopic dimensions, enabling us to convey to a small area at a great distance trillions of times more energy than is possible with rays of any kind. Many thousands of horsepower can be thus transmitted by a stream thinner than a hair, so that nothing can resist."

Apparently what Tesla had in mind with this defensive system was a large-scale version of his Colorado Springs lightning bolt machine. As airplanes or ships entered the electric field of his charged tower, they would set up a conducting path for a stream of high-energy particles that would destroy the intruder's electrical system.

A drawback to having giant Tesla transmitters poised to shoot bolts of lightning at an enemy approaching the coasts is that they would have to be located in an uninhabited area equal to its circle of protection. Anyone stepping into the defensive zone of the coils would be sensed as an intruder and struck down.

Electricity For Peace Or War?

As ominous as Death Ray and beam weapon technology will be for the future, there is another, more destructive; weapon system alluded to in Tesla's writings. This system could either deliver electricity without the need for wires, or act as a weapon of unimaginable destruction.

When Tesla realized, as he pointed out in an article published in 1900 in *Century Magazine*, that "economic forces would not allow the development of a new type of electrical generator able to supply power without burning fuel. I am led to recognize [that] the transmission of electrical energy to any distance through the media as by far the best solution of the great problem of harnessing the sun's energy for the use of man."

His idea was that a relatively few generating plants located near waterfalls would supply his very high energy transmitters which, in turn, would send power through the earth to be picked up wherever it was needed. The plan would require several of his transmitters to rhythmically pump huge amounts of electricity into the earth at pressures on the order of 100 million volts. The earth would become like a huge ball inflated to a great electrical potential, but pulsing to Tesla's imposed beat.

Receiving energy from this high-pressure reservoir only would require a person to put a rod into the ground and connect it to a receiver operating in unison with the earth's electrical motion.

As Tesla described it, "the entire apparatus for lighting the average country dwelling will contain no moving parts whatever, and could be readily carried about in a small valise."

NIKOLA TESLA'S DEATH RAY AND THE
COLUMBIA SPACE SHUTTLE DISASTER

Tesla said his transmitter could produce 100 million volts of pressure with currents up to 1000 amperes, which is a power level of 100 billion watts. If it were resonating at a radio frequency of 2 MHz, then the energy released during one period of its oscillation would be 100,000,000,000,000,000 Joules of energy, roughly the amount of energy released by the explosion of 10 megatons of TNT.

Such a transmitter would be capable of projecting the energy of a nuclear warhead by radio. Any location in the world could be vaporized into atomic dust at the speed of light.

Not unexpectedly, many scientists doubted the technical feasibility of Tesla's wireless power transmission scheme whether for commercial or military purposes. Some engineers were working for companies that had financial interests in making sure that wireless electricity did not become a reality, so naturally they did not give the idea a fair shake. However, the secret of through-the-earth broadcast power was found not in the theories of electrical engineering, but in the realm of high energy physics.

Dr. Andrija Puharich, in 1976, was the first to point out that Tesla's power transmission system could not be explained by the laws of classical electrodynamics, but, rather, in terms of relativistic transformations in high energy fields.

He noted that according to Dirac's theory of the electron, when one of those particles encountered its oppositely charged member, a positron, the two particles would annihilate each other. Because energy can neither be destroyed nor created, the energy of the two former particles are transformed into an electromagnetic wave.

The opposite, of course, holds true. If there is a strong enough electric field, two opposite charges of electricity are formed where there was originally no charge at all. This type of transformation usually takes place near the intense field near an atomic nucleus, but it can also manifest without the aid of a nuclear catalyst if an electric field has enough energy. Puharich's extremely involved mathematical treatment demonstrated that power levels in a Tesla transmitter were strong enough to cause such pair production.

The mechanism of pair production offers a very attractive explanation for the ground transmission of power. Ordinary electrical currents do not travel far through the earth. Dirt has a high resistance to electricity and quickly turns currents into heat energy that is wasted. With the pair production method electricity can be moved from one point to another without really having to push the physical particle through the earth; the transmitting source would create a strong field, and a particle would be created at the receiver.

In 1908, Tesla revealed in an article for **Electrical Hobbyist Magazine** the destructive effects of his energy transmitter. His Wardenclyffe transmitter was much larger than the Colorado Springs device that destroyed the power station's generator. This new transmitter would be capable of effects many orders of magnitude greater than the Colorado device. In 1915, he said he had already built a transmitter that "when unavoidable, may be used to destroy property and life."

Finally, a 1934 letter from Tesla to J.P. Morgan, uncovered by Tesla biographer Margaret Cheney, seems to conclusively point to successful energy weapon tests. In an effort to raise money for his defensive system he wrote: "The flying machine has completely demoralized the world, so much so that in some cities, as London and Paris, people are in mortal fear from aerial bombing. The new means I have perfected affords absolute protection against this and other forms of attack ... These new discoveries I have carried out experimentally on a limited scale, created a profound impression."

Marconi's Wave Gun

In her autobiography, Rachele Mussolini, the wife of Italian fascist dictator Benito Mussolini, detailed a fascinating account of Guglielmo Marconi's demonstration of a device that could stop vehicles cold from a distance.

In June of 1936 Marconi demonstrated to Italian fascist dictator Benito Mussolini a wave gun device that could be used as a defensive weapon. In the 1930s such devices were popularized as death rays as in a Boris Karloff film of the same name. Marconi demonstrated the ray on a busy highway north of Milan one afternoon. Mussolini had asked his wife Rachele to also be on the highway at precisely 3:30 in the afternoon. Marconi's device caused the electrical systems in all the cars, including Rachele's, to malfunction for half an hour, while her chauffeur and other motorists checked their fuel pumps and spark plugs. At 3:35 all the cars were able to start again.

Marconi's wave gun device was just one of many "high tech" devices for warfare that were being researched during that time. The British government was busy putting together teams of scientists to look into the possibilities of producing Death Rays that could potentially be used against attacking aircraft.

The Director of Scientific Research in the Air Ministry had enough concern about the possibility of attack from the air and the consequences thereof, that he set up a committee to "...consider how far recent advances in scientific and technical knowledge can be used to strengthen the present methods of defense against hostile aircraft"

Henry T. Tizard, Chairman of the Aeronautical Research Committee, would chair this new committee, which was to be called the Scientific Survey of Air Defense. Tizard turned for advice to Robert Alexander Watson-Watt, Superintendent of the Radio Research Station.

Tizard and Wimperis put the question to him: 'Could such a Death Ray be constructed and used against enemy aircraft?' Watson-Watt put this question of whether a Death Ray could be built or not to one of the members of his staff at NPL, Arnold F. Wilkins who was charged with calculating how much energy would be required to damage an aircraft, or its crew, and if such a ray was possible could it have already been produced? Wilkins investigated the possibility of such a ray and concluded that while in theory it was possible, the power required to make it effective would be so prohibitively high that he considered it quite impossible that such a device could be built.

Arnold Wilkins reported his findings back to Robert Watson-Watt and the two men concluded that in effect this was what they had expected. Watson-Watt reported back on February 4 1935, to Tizard and Wimperis that there was no possibility of a high energy ray harming the aircraft or the aircrew.

Nevertheless, the original research that had been conducted to see if a Death Ray was possible did lead to an exciting discovery. British Post Office engineers had noticed that an aircraft, flying through an experimental high frequency beam, had caused the beam to 'flutter' a noticeable degree. The matter had been reported in a Post Office report, which, while it had not received wide circulation, had come to the attention of Arnold Wilkins who had been working at the time with Watson-Watt at the Radio Research Station.

Wilkins remembered this report and thought that it might be used as the basis of a system for detecting aircraft. Watson-Watt was sufficiently interested to ask him to calculate the possibility of using this and, after some work, Wilkins came back with the conclusion that it was quite possible to develop some form of aircraft detection system given the right equipment. It seemed that the probability of an aircraft, re-radiating a radio signal aimed at it back to the source, was very high.

Robert Watson-Watt drew up a document of the results of Arnold Wilkins' work to report back to Tizard, Wimperis and Rowe on Tuesday, 12 February 1935. The report was entitled *The Detection and Location of Aircraft by Radio Means*, and in it Watson-Watt wrote his now famous memorandum that "Although it was impossible to destroy aircraft by means of radio waves, it should be possible to detect them by radio energy bouncing back from the aircraft's body"

Even though this particular line of research did not lead to the development of a functional Death Ray, it did lead to the creation of one of the greatest achievements in modern technology, RADAR.

In the 1940's anti-personnel electromagnetic weapons were referenced in the U.S. Strategic Bombing Survey (*Pacific Survey, Military Analy-*

sis Division, Volume 63), which reviewed Japanese research and development efforts on a Death Ray.

Whilst not reaching the stage of practical application, research was considered to be sufficiently promising to warrant the expenditure of two million Yen during the years 1940-1945. Deep in the paper halls of the Nohorito Laboratory the designs for this new weapon were conceived using very short radio waves focused into a high power beam. Summarizing the Japanese efforts, allied scientists concluded that a ray apparatus might be developed that could kill unshielded human beings at a distance of five to 10 miles.

Although the Death Ray weapon was rudimentary, enough research had been done by the Nohorito Laboratory to not dismiss such a weapon in the future. The Scientific Advisory Group went on to hint in their report that the U.S. military should continue research with this Death Ray weapon.

Studies demonstrated that, for example, automobile engines could be stopped by tuned waves as early as 1943. It is, therefore, reasonable to suopose that this technique has been available for a great many years.

NIKOLA TESLA'S DEATH RAY AND THE
COLUMBIA SPACE SHUTTLE DISASTER

Research on living organisms (mice and ground hogs) revealed that waves from two meters to 60 centimeters in length caused hemorrhage of lungs, whereas waves shorter than two meters destroyed brain cells.

There were only two major drawbacks to the Japanese Death Ray. First, the participant being subjected to the ray needed to remain stationary. Secondly, it took a full ten minutes for the Death Ray to be effective. The report concluded that: "the experiments indicate progress and if continued, probably would lead to the development of a death-dealing ray reaching greater distances."

Germany, as well, was conducting its own Death Ray experiments; in fact, it is believed that Nazi spies stationed in Manhattan managed to steal important notes dealing with the Death Ray from the apartment of Nikola Tesla. In April 1943, Robert Ley, Minister for Labor in Nazi Germany, excitedly told Albert Speer that German scientists had invented a Death Ray.

Ley said that physicist Sir James Chadwick invented the Death Ray in the 1930's and that Nazi scientists had just recently perfected it. The Nazi Death Ray was allegedly a neutron beam that would collide with a uranium or fissile target and produce a controlled nuclear reaction.

Hitler may have intended to activate his nuclear Death Ray in 1944, when he ordered the destruction of Paris. But the sabotage of a key pipeline bridge postponed such action. The Allies landed in Europe before the Death Ray could be functional again and it was forced to shut down in 1945. However, its location was never disclosed.

Captain Heinze Schaeffer, captain of the U-977 submarine stated in his book, **Uboat 977**, that in April, 1945 an S.S. associate had offered him a demonstration of a socalled Death Ray. Schaeffer had to decline the offer in order to make his famous last voyage across the Atlantic before the final German downfall.

NIKOLA TESLA'S DEATH RAY AND THE
COLUMBIA SPACE SHUTTLE DISASTER

Tesla in his laboratory surrounded by lightning.

Chapter Eight

Further Evidence of Modern Death Rays

In the twentieth century a new technology called Focused Electromagnetic Broadcasting has been developed that is startling in its power and implications. These weapons are part of the new "non-lethal" arsenal—a misnomer, since this weaponry might just as well be called a Death Ray—touted by the military as a humane way for conducting war in the years to come. It may also be a way of conducting "peace" of the 1984 and Brave New World mind-controlled variety.

Certainly this possibility has not been over-looked, as evidenced by the following quote from Zbigniew Brzezinski, in his *Between Two Ages: Ametica's Role in the Technetronic Era*: "It may be possible, and tempting, to exploit for strategic political purposed the fruits of research on the brain and on human behavior. Gordon J.F. MacDonald, a geophysicist specializing in problems of warfare, has written that artificially excited electronic strokes 'could lead to a pattern of oscillations that produce relatively high power levels over certain regions of the earth ... In this way, one could develop a system that would seriously impair the brain performance of very large populations in selected regions over an extended period.' No matter how deeply disturbing the thought of using the environment to manipulate behavior for national advantages to some, the technology permitting such use will very probably develop within the next few decades."

In 1965 the McFarlane Corporation in America came up with the science fiction sounding "modulated electron gun X-ray nuclear booster," a breakthrough in the Death Ray technology. Reports indicate that the device could also be used in communications, telemetry, and remote controlled guidance systems. McFarlane later claimed that NASA stole the system and that the principles were used in the MIROS communications satellite.

The Moscow Death Beam

In 1960 there were rumors of a fantastic new Soviet super weapon employing Nikola Tesla electromagnetic technology. With subsequent revelations about Soviet research in these areas, it seems that these rumors were true.

NIKOLA TESLA'S DEATH RAY AND THE
COLUMBIA SPACE SHUTTLE DISASTER

During the 1960s high levels of electromagnetic radiation were detected at the American embassy in Moscow. It was determined that the face of the embassy was being systematically swept with electromagnetic emissions by the Soviets.

One guess was that a microwave beam was used to activate electronic equipment hidden within the building; another guess was more macabre: that the beam was being used to disrupt the nervous systems of American workers in the embassy.

Giving weight to the latter supposition, many Of the employees of the embassy became ill. Ambassador Walter Stoessel suffered a rare blood disease likened to leukemia, and experienced headaches and bleeding from the eyes. At least two other employees contracted cancer. According to researcher Alex Constantine, rather than informing embassy personnel of what was going on, the CIA chose to study the effects of the radiation.

Dr. Milton Zaret, called in to investigate what was termed "the Moscow Signal," reported that the CIA wondered, "whether I thought the electromagnetic radiation beamed at the brain from a distance could affect the way a person might act," and, "could microwaves be used to facilitate brainwashing or to break down prisoners under investigation."

Zaret's conclusion about the Moscow Signal was that, "Whatever other reasons the Russians may have had, they believed the beam would modify the behavior of personnel."

Author Len Bracken, who was present in Moscow at the time, reported to the late author Jim Keith that the microwave radiation was beamed from a shack on a building across from the embassy. In 1977 the microwave shack caught fire and burned. Bracken also relates that "in '79 a strange box was installed in the wall in my room [in Moscow], supposedly relating to the heating system."

Irradiation of the American embassy reportedly prompted a response from the Americans: the Defense Advanced Research Projects Agency's Project PANDORA, conducted at the Walter Reed Army Institute of Research from 1965 to 1970. One aspect of the project involved bombarding chimpanzees with microwave radiation. Referencing a reported statement by the head of the project, "the potential for exerting a degree of control on human behavior by low level microwave radiation seems to exist and he urged that the effects of microwaves be studied for possible weapons applications."

Within three years, Dr. Gordon J. F. McDonald, a scientific advisor to the president at the time reported, "Perturbation of the environment can produce changes in behavioral patterns." The perturbation that McDonald was alluding to was EM waves, and the changes in behavior were altered brain wave patterns.

That the electromagnetic arsenal is being used against citizenry in Russia is quite apparent from a statement published at the end of 1991 by SovData Dialine: "Psychological warfare is still being used by state security agents against people in Russia, even after the abortive August coup," said Emilia Chirkova, a Deputy of the Zelenograd Soviet and member of the Human Rights Conmission.

She recalls the scandal surrounding the alleged bugging equipment installed close to Boris Yeltsin's office. KGB agents admitted then that the directional aerial in the equipment was designed for transmission, not for reception. She believes it was part of an attempt to affect the health of the Russian president using high frequency electromagnetic radiation. "The Human Rights Committee," Chirkova said, "had warned Yeltsin about such a possibility."

Victor Sedleckij, design engineer-in-chief for the center Forma and vice president of the League of Independent Soviet Scientists provided substantiation for Chirkova's allegations. Aedleckij stated, "In Kiev was launched a mass production of psychotronic biogenerators and their tests. I cannot assert that during the [Moscow] coup d'etat those used were the Kiev generators ... All the same, that [psychotronic generators] were used is evident to me. What are the psychotronic generators? They are electronic equipment that produces the effect of guided control in human organisms. It affects especially the left and right hemisphere of the cortex. This is also the technology of the U.S. Project Zombie 5 ... I draw on my personal experience since I am myself the designer of such a generator."

Emilia Chirkova cited several instances of the use of similar devices. Microwave equipment had been used in 1989 and 1990 in Vladivostok and Moscow prisons, in a mental hospital in Oryol, and in the Serbsky Institute in Moscow [also a mental hospital], she said.

During his exile in Gorky, Andrei Sakharov noticed the presence of a high-tension electromagnetic field in his flat. It was reported recently in the press that Ruslan Khasbulatov, Speaker of the Russian Parliament, had to move from his flat to another district of Moscow. High-level electro-magnetic radiation has been included among the possible causes of the discomfort he felt in his flat.

Purported victims of psychological warfare have written to Russian newspapers complaining about the use of Death Rays on them by the government. From Voronezh: "They controlled my laughter, my thoughts, and caused pain in various parts of my body... It all started in October 1985, after I had openly criticized the first secretary of the City Committee of the Communist Party."

"Sometimes voices can be heard in the head from the effect of microwave pulse radiation which causes acoustic oscillations in the brain," explained Gennady Shchelkunov, a radio electronics researcher from the Istok Association. In June 1991, a group of Zelenograd deputies sent an appeal signed by 150 people to President Yeltsin, demanding an investigation into the use of bio-electronic weapons.

NIKOLA TESLA'S DEATH RAY AND THE COLUMBIA SPACE SHUTTLE DISASTER

Human Experiments By The Military

In 1972 the army admitted extensive research into the effects of irradiation on life forms, and the technology of electromagnetic weaponry. One of the by products of this research led to the invention of a powerful "electronic flame thrower." This may have been the weapon described in a study of the U.S. Army Mobility Equipment Research and Development Center, *Analysis of Microwaves for Barrier Warfare*, describing the use of electromagnetic energy for an anti-personnel and vehicle weapon. The weapon discussed in this study was stated to be capable of producing third degree burns on human skin.

Dr. Dietrich Beischer, a German scientist employed by the American government, irradiated 7,000 naval crewmen with potentially harmful levels of microwave energy at the naval Aerospace Research Laboratory in Pensacola, Florida, and talked about it at a symposium in 1973. Dr. Beischer disappeared soon after the experiment.

According to PANDORA alumnus Robert O. Becker, he was to spend some time with Beischer but, "Just before the meeting, I got a call from him. With no preamble or explanation, he blurted out: 'I'm at a pay phone. I can't talk long. They are watching me. I can't come to the meeting or ever communicate with you again. I'm sorry. You've been a good friend. Goodby.' Soon afterward I called his office at Pensacola and was told, 'I'm sorry, there is no one here by that name.' Just as in the movies. A guy who had done important research there for decades just disappeared."

According to Eldon Byrd, of the Naval Surface Weapons Center in Silver Springs, Maryland, "Between 1981 and September 1982, the Navy commissioned me to investigate the potential of developing electromagnetic devices that could be used as non-lethal weapons by the Marine Corps for the purpose of 'riot control,' hostage removal, embassy and ship security, clandestine operations, and so on."

Byrd wrote of experiments in irradiating animals with low level electromagnetic fields, mentioning changes in brain function, and stating that the animals "exhibited a drastic degradation of intelligence later in life ... couldn't learn easy tasks ... indicating a very definite and irreversible damage to the central nervous system of the fetus."

By the early 1970s, according to Robert C. Beck, "Anecdotal data amassed suggesting that a pocket-sized transmitter at power levels of under 100 milliwatts could drastically alter the moods of unsuspecting persons, and that vast geographical areas could be surreptitiously mood manipulated by invisible and remote transmissions of EM [electromagnetic] energy."

In the late 1970s Russian negotiators at the Strategic Arms Limitation talks (SALT II), proposed banning "a new generation of weapons of mass destruction" employing electromagnetic pulses. It has been suggested that the Russians, in proposing the ban, were attempting to feel out the Americans as to the current state of their electromagnetic weapons research. The Americans did not seem to have a clue as to what the Russians were talking about, and the proposal was tabled.

In fact, some Americans knew exactly what the Russians were talking about - in 1959 Russian scientists Gaponov, Schneider, and Pantell had conceived of what was called a cyclotron resonance maser, essentially an industrial strength tunable ray gun. Beginning about 1966, the Russians launched into a heavily funded crash project to develop the gyrotron, another form of electromagnetic gun, and in 1971 they were engaged in their first field tests with the gyrotron.

NIKOLA TESLA'S DEATH RAY AND THE COLUMBIA SPACE SHUTTLE DISASTER

In 1975, physicists M. S. Rabinovich and A. A. Rukhadze and others active in Russian strategic defense at the Lebedev Physics Institute in Moscow announced that using a cyclotron resonance maser, they had produced microwave bursts that far outstripped anything the Americans were even theoretically proposing and that, according to the analysis of the American military, were powerful enough to be used in weapons applications.

A report from the American Rand Corporation at the time concluded that the Russian experiments were part of a larger Russian program designed for the production of electromagnetic weaponry, centered at the Institute of Applied Physics in Gorkey, Lebedev Physics Institute in Moscow, and another group of research institutes in Tomsk. By the 1980s, it was reported, Russian gyrotron weapons had been reduced in size so that they would fit into a regular military truck, and had the capability of wiping out large military emplacements or, at lower frequencies, irradiating whole towns.

In 1982 the Air Force released a review of the use of electromagnetics on life forms, saying, "Currently available data allow the projection that specially generated radio frequency radiation (RFR) fields may pose powerful and revolutionary antipersonnel military threats. Electroshock therapy indicates the ability of induced electric current to completely interrupt mental functioning for short periods of time, to obtain cognition for longer periods and to restructure emotional response over prolonged intervals. Impressed electromagnetic fields can be disruptive to purposeful behavior and may be capable of directing and/or interrogating such behavior.

Further, the passage of approximately 100 milliamperes through the myocardium can lead to cardiac standstill and death, again pointing to a speed-of-light weapons effect. A rapidly scanning RFR system could provide an effective stun or kill capability over a large area.

In 1984 the program researching the creation of pulsed microwaves was stepped up at Lawrence Livermore National Laboratories. According to the **Oregon Journal**, in March 1978, in a story titled *Mysterious Radio Signals Causing Concern*, the city of Eugene was irradiated by microwaves possibly beamed from a Navy transmitter, located several hundred miles away in California. According to an FCC report, "microwaves were the likely cause of several sudden illnesses among faculty researchers at Oregon

State University." Numerous residents also complained of headaches, insomnia, fatigue, skin redness, and hearing clicks and buzzes in the head.

A study conducted by the Pacific Northwest Center for Non-Ionizing Radiation attributed the radiation instead to the Soviets, stating that it was "psychoactive" and "very strongly suggesting of achieving the objective of either physical harm or brain control."

In September 1985, members of the Greenharn Commons Women's Peace Camp in Great Britain, a global militarization protest camp located outside the U.S. Air Force Base at Greenharn Commons, began experiencing a wide range of unpleasant physical symptoms including headache, depression, disorientation, memory loss, vertigo, and changes in their menstrual cycles.

According to Dr. Rosalie Bertell and others who researched what was going on, the symptoms were of the type associated with exposure to radiation, and they began shortly after security at the base was switched from human guards to primarily electronic surveillance—this would have been a perfect opportunity to install electromagnetic broadcasting units disguised as surveillance equipment.

Dr. Bertell, former radar engineer Kim Besly, and others took readings of electromagnetic levels in the area, and found that they were as much as 100 times as strong as other nearby areas.

A recent news release provides information on a new program by the National Institute of Justice, to develop "friendly force" electromagnetic weapons for use in the U.S. According to Microwave News, Oak Ridge National Laboratory is looking into the possibility of Death Ray "thermal guns" that would disable an individual by causing his body to overheat, "seizure guns" that would induce epileptic fits, and "magnetosphere guns" that would cause a person to "see stars."

But quite how close such weapons are to reality we may never know. The U.S. National Academy of Sciences is refusing to release dozens of reports proposing or describing their development, even though the documents are supposed to be public records.

The academy is justifying its unprecedented reticence by citing security concerns after 9/11. But campaigners think the real reason is that the research violates both U.S. law and international treaties on chemical and biological weapons.

NIKOLA TESLA'S DEATH RAY AND THE COLUMBIA SPACE SHUTTLE DISASTER

One group at Oak Ridge National Laboratory in Tennessee, for example, proposes using intense electromagnetic fields to produce effects "ranging from the disruption of short-term memory to total loss of control of voluntary bodily functions." Others propose directed energy weapons, or Death Rays.

The idea of weapons like these being used in warfare is disturbing enough, but what if terrorists get their hands on them? According to Bill Radasky, an expert in electromagnetic interference with Metatech in Goleta, California, they may have already done so. A basic microwave weapon, he says, can be cobbled together with bits from an electrical store for just a few hundred dollars. Such a system would be small enough to fit in the back of a car and could crash a computer from 100 meters away.

Other systems are even easier to acquire. Some mail-order electronics outlets sell compact microwave sources that are designed to test the vulnerability of electronics. But they could just as easily be used in anger.

"We've done experiments that show it's very easy to do," says Radasky. "We've damaged a lot of equipment with those little boxes and with the right kind of hardware they could be used to hurt or even kill people."

The Tesla Earthquake Weapon

Tesla energy weapons allegedly can also be used to induce earthquakes in susceptible areas. As mentioned earlier in this book, the Japanese Cult Aum Shinrikyo is thought to have been intimately involved in the development of futuristic doomsday weapons based on Tesla technology. These weapons are so advanced that they don't 'officially' exist in the armories of the major powers. They include the use of electromagnetic pulse, earthquake inducing and plasma weapons being covertly tested in remote regions of the world.

At the center of these allegations are a series of powerful earthquakes, strange fireballs and aerial lights manifesting above Western Australia. They also revolve around the major January 1995 quake that laid waste to the Japanese City of Kobe. Suggestions that the Kobe earthquake may have been caused by a Tesla-Energy Powered seismic weapon continue to circulate among defense circles.

Extraordinarily, the Kobe quake was predicted nine days before the event by Aum's charismatic guru Shoko Asahara. In a radio broadcast on January 8 1995, Asahara stated: "Japan will be attacked by an earthquake in 1995. The most likely place is Kobe."

Hideo Murai, the late Science and Technology minister for Aum Shinrikyo also adhered to this view, answering questions about the Kobe quake in a news conference at the Foreign Correspondent Club in Japan on April 7 1995, Murai said: "There is a strong possibility of the activation of an earthquake using electromagnetic power, or somebody might have used a device that applied force inside the Earth."

The Aum leadership believed the Kobe quake to be an act of war. "Kobe was hit by a surprise attack," they claimed, adding that the city was an "appropriate guinea pig." Murai, said to have been the most intelligent Japanese who ever lived, was murdered in a Yakuza orchestrated assassination shortly after speaking to foreign news correspondents.

U.S. Senate Investigates Allegations of Earthquake Weaponry used in Kobe

Aum's interest in weapons of mass destruction was considered serious enough to merit the launch of a special investigation by the U.S. Senate Permanent Subcommittee on Investigations.

NIKOLA TESLA'S DEATH RAY AND THE COLUMBIA SPACE SHUTTLE DISASTER

Chaired by Senator Sam Nunn, the committee spent five months conducting hundreds of interviews of "government and private individuals" and included classified briefings from numerous U.S. intelligence agencies. Their 100-page report was published in October 1995.

The Nunn Report revealed the cult's fascination for so-called Tesla Weapons and mentions Tesla's development of a "Death Ray in the 1930's, which was actually a particle beam accelerator," and which was said to be able to "shoot down an airplane at 200 miles." Aum personnel also traveled to the Tesla Museum in Belgrade to research the so-called Tesla Coil—a device used for amplifying alternating currents— and uncovered Tesla's work on "high energy voltage transmission and wave amplification, which Tesla asserted could be used to create seismological disturbances."

A Final Word

Here is another bit of food for thought. There is a verse in the Old Testament book Obadiah that has been interpreted in the past as a warning about mankind's efforts to put himself into space.

In Obadiah, which consists of only one chapter, verse four reads: "Though you soar aloft like the eagle, though your nest is among the stars, thence I will bring you down."

The reader should remember that as Apollo I I first touched down on the moon in July of 1969, the rapt worldwide audience heard the words "The Eagle has landed." It is easy enough to see that the space shuttle program could be what is intended by the second part of the verse that reads, "Though your nest is among the stars."

Perhaps the God of the Bible, who is himself often regarded as an alien entity, has issued a dire warning about the effrontery of his creation trying to conquer space through his own scientific devices. Maybe we are being told that sometimes outer space is off limits to God's unruly child, mankind.

The many questions posed by the Columbia disaster will most likely remain unanswered. Whether it was Nikola Tesla's Death Ray in the hands of an enemy country or even high-tech renegade terrorists, or an alien force bent on reining in our progress on the frontiers of outer space, or simply a tragic human error that has yet to surface in NASA's ongoing investigation of the cause of the crash, the mystery of just what happened to Columbia will continue to haunt us for a long time to come.

NIKOLA TESLA'S DEATH RAY AND THE COLUMBIA SPACE SHUTTLE DISASTER

For other books and videos about Nikola Tesla,
write for your free catalog:
**GLOBAL COMMUNICATION P.O. BOX 753
NEW, BRUNSWICK, NJ 08903**
Visit the Conspiracy Journal website:
www.conspiracyjournal.com

NIKOLA TESLA'S DEATH RAY AND THE COLUMBIA SPACE SHUTTLE DISASTER

NIKOLA TESLA'S DEATH RAY AND THE COLUMBIA SPACE SHUTTLE DISASTER